Death or Dialogue?

Gott.
5
15
16 - 18

Knitter   19 - 42

Death or Dialogue?

From the Age of Monologue
to the Age of Dialogue

—

Leonard Swidler

John B. Cobb Jr

Paul F. Knitter

Monica K. Hellwig

SCM Press · London
Trinity Press International · Philadelphia

First published 1990

SCM Press Ltd
26–30 Tottenham Road
London N1 4BZ

Trinity Press International
3725 Chestnut Street
Philadelphia, Pa. 19104

British Library Cataloguing in Publication Data

Death or dialogue?
1. Religions. Interactions
I. Cobb, John B. (John Boswell)
291.172
ISBN 0–334–02445–5

Library of Congress Cataloging-in-Publication Data

Death or dialogue? : from the age of monologue to the age
    of dialogue
/John B. Cobb. Jr. . . . [et al.].
    p.   cm.
   ISBN 0–334–02445–5 : $15.95
    1. Religions – Relations. 2. Christianity and other
    religions.
    3. Disputations, Religious. 4. Dialogue – Religious
    aspects.
I. Cobb, John B.
BL410.D42 1990
291.1′72–dc20   90–31485

Typeset at The Spartan Press Ltd, Lymington, Hants
and printed in Great Britain by
Richard Clay Ltd, Bungay, Suffolk

Contents

Introduction

The future offers two alternatives: death or dialogue. This statement is not over-dramatization. In the past it was possible, indeed, unavoidable, for most human beings to live out their lives in isolation from the vast majority of their fellows, without even having a faint awareness of, let alone interest in, their very existence. At most, and for most, the occasional tale with distorted descriptions of distant denizens whiled away their moments of leisure and satisfied their curiosity. Everyone for the most part talked to their own cultural selves. Even the rare descriptions of "the other" hardly ever came from "the other" themselves, but from some of their own who had heard, or heard of, "the other." Put briefly, until the edge of the present era, humans lived in the Age of Monologue. That age is now passing.

We are now poised at the entrance to the Age of Dialogue. We travel all over the globe, and large elements of the entire globe come to us. There can hardly be a campus which does not echo with foreign accents and languages. Our streets, businesses and homes are visibly filled with overseas products. We constantly hear about the crises of our massive trade deficit and the overwhelming debts Second- and Third-World countries owe us. Through our Asian-made television sets we invite into our living rooms myriads of people of strange nations, cultures and religions. We can no longer ignore "the other," but we can close our minds and spirits to them, look at them with fear and misunderstanding, come to resent them, and perhaps even hate them. This way of encounter leads to hostility and eventually war and death. For example, one of the fundamental reasons why Japan attacked Pearl Harbor in 1941 was because the Japanese leadership perceived the US moves as a basic economic threat to their wellbeing. The American response eventually was to drop atomic bombs on "the Japs," annihilating hundreds of thousands of human beings in two brief instants.

Today nuclear or ecological, or other, catastrophic devastation lies just a little way further down the path of monologue. It is only by struggling out of the self-centered monologic mindset into dialogue with "the others" as they really are, and not as we have projected them in our monologues, that we can avoid such cataclysmic disasters. In brief: we must move from the Age of Monologue to the Age of Dialogue.

What we understand to be the explanation of the ultimate meaning of life, and how to live accordingly, is what we call our religion – or if that explanation is not based on a notion of the transcendent, we can call it an ideology. Since our religion or ideology is so comprehensive, so all-inclusive, it is the most fundamental area in which "the other" is likely to be different from us – and hence possibly seen as the most threatening. Again, this is not over-dramatization. The current catalogue of conflicts which have religion/ideology as a constituent element is staggering, including such obvious neuralgic flashpoints as Northern Ireland, Lebanon, Israel, Sri Lanka, Pakistan/India, Afghanistan – to say nothing of "atheistic Marxism" versus the "Christian West"!

Hence, if humankind is to move from the Age of Monologue into the Age of Dialogue, the religions and ideologies must enter into the movement full force. We have in fact begun to make serious progress along this path, though the journey stretches far ahead. As a contribution to moving humankind along this journey with as little stumbling and as rapid progress as possible, four of us Christian theologians who for years have been struggling along the uncharted path of dialogue here try to set out some guideposts for our fellows. We fully realize that we are not infallible guides, but we hope that others might learn from our trial-and-error experience and constant reflection on how best to go along the path of dialogue.

Because we four are Christians, we speak in the first place to our fellow Christians, but we would be pleased if others also found some help in our lines here set down. Each of us lays out our understanding of what interreligious, interideological dialogue is, what its goals and means are, why specifically we Christians ought to enter into dialogue and how we can handle the traditional Christian claims to the exclusive and universal means of "salvation." Each of us also exemplifies concretely that theoretical reflection by explicating a traditionally exclusivistic text from the Christian scriptures or tradition. But perhaps most important of all, we attempt not only to tell you our readers *about* dialogue, but also show you dialogue in action. Thus, we hope that you will do as we do, even if you do not always do as we say.

Leonard Swidler

Dialogue

—

John B. Cobb, Jr

I. Confrontation and dialogue

Much of our communication with one another moves between the poles of confrontation and dialogue. Confrontation is an essential element in communication. People are not likely to hear what others are saying unless they are brought up short, unless they realize that something is being said to them that differs from what they already know, that conflicts with existing opinions and perceptions. Otherwise, we are all prone to reinterpret what we hear to fit with what we already believe. Sometimes confrontation can be effective only if it is backed by force or the threat of force, only if it actually stops normal activities and thus gains attention to what is being said.

But confrontation alone is not the answer. In extreme cases it may overpower the one who is confronted. Student demonstrations have brought down governments. Some people simply crumble psychologically when confronted. The formerly dominant one may become submissive. Or a confrontation by force may simply destroy what is confronted. Sometimes the changes effected by such confrontation may be improvements, but more often they are not. The world cannot operate by confrontation alone.

Confrontation can contribute reliably to real gains only when it leads to dialogue. If it succeeds in getting attention, and if then the two sides listen to each other and explain themselves to each other, there is a chance of a change that destroys neither. It may even be that in the end both are better satisfied. That is, at any rate, the goal and hope.

Christians have engaged, and continue to engage, in a great deal of confrontation. That is good and right. Christians legitimately believe that the prophetic message and the gospel are worthy of attention by all. They fail in their obedience if they do not proclaim the truth that has been entrusted to them. The powers and principalities of this world must be confronted. Injustice and oppression must be named for what they are, and those who perpetuate them must be confronted. The same applies to superstition and magic. The problem with the old-line churches is more often that they confront too little than that they confront too much. The image of the church militant has its place.

In the history of the church, confrontation has played a large role. It has been a powerful force. Before it, whole systems of thought and life have crumbled. The church militant has often been the church triumphant.

Today, as we look back, we are not as proud of these accomplishments as we once were. We see that what crumbled and was lost was not without its own value. We see that the Christian institutions and beliefs that replaced it have been highly ambiguous. What we once confidently considered progress, now seems mixed. We wonder how pleased Jesus would have been about the ways in which we have extended the church and the effects it has had on cultures and individuals. Hence we ask, was it right to work with confrontation alone? Or should we have used confrontation as the first step toward dialogue? A new consensus has emerged that it is better to listen as well as to speak.

To supplement confrontation with dialogue means that one believes that what is confronted is not simply an embodiment of evil. Oppressors, for example, are not only oppressors. They are also children of God caught in social processes, with needs and fears and concerns that should be heard. There may still be times when the destruction of oppressors is the best that can be attained. But the norm is the change of the pattern of relationships so that the human needs of the erstwhile oppressors are also met. That requires that the oppressors be heard as well as addressed.

If that is so even with oppressors, is it not *a fortiori* the case when we deal with those who live nobly and idealistically out of great traditions that have derived from saints and sages? Surely the answer is, Yes!, and there is a growing consensus among Christians to that effect. We cannot have dialogue without confrontation, for others must understand that we have something to say to them. But sheer confrontation directed to their destruction, or to the destruction of the wisdom they embody, no longer seems faithful to Christ. We confront with the conviction that others have something to say to us – that we need to listen as well as speak.

II. Dialogue and its dangers

Still, there is a deep uneasiness about listening too intently, too expectantly, too openly. Might we not hear ideas that are in conflict with our deepest convictions? How can we be open to those? Do we not need, before entering into dialogue, to clarify the non-negotiable elements in our own faith, so that we can be clear about that to which we can be open and that which is beyond the pale?

In the case of dialogue with oppressors there is the danger that sympathetic attention to their needs may lead to acquiescence in structures that continue to oppress. In the case of dialogue with believers in other traditions there is danger that sympathetic appreciation of their concerns may lead to compromise of faith itself. In leaping out of the frying pan of sheer confrontation may we not be leaping into the fire of relativism and unbelief?

The dangers are very real, and they always will be. Human life does not offer recipes for attaining purity and perfection. The issue is not whether dialogue can have destructive effects. The issue is whether it is inherent in dialogue, as it is inherent in confrontation by itself, to have destructive effects. I believe not. I believe that when dialogue functions fully, when it is not distorted, its results are healthy and fulfilling to all involved. Of course, it will always be distorted in part, so one may complain that the presentation of an ideal as non-destructive is irrelevant. But that is to misunderstand. We are not seeking perfection in this world. But we are seeking to find those avenues whose pursuit has promise for reducing the world's evil. Those avenues are the ones that are inherently positive. That we will fail to follow them perfectly is not a reason to abandon the effort.

Consider the nature of dialogue more closely. It begins with confrontation. Both partners must realize that there are differences between them and be prepared to take these differences seriously. That involves having the position of the partner explained more carefully. One needs to say what one thinks one has heard and have that checked. In the process one usually finds that beliefs that initially seemed wholly antithetical are less so. What initially sounded outrageous or absurd, when better understood, has some plausibility.

A dialogue may end there, with the partners understanding one another better. Usually that means that they also respect one another more. They see that there may be areas of agreement between them and can look forward to possible cooperation. That is a gain.

When practical issues are immediately at stake, when some action must be taken, dialogue cannot stop with mutual understanding. There must be a decision. Perhaps the best that can be attained is a compromise with which both partners are dissatisfied. Even so, it is likely that the compromise is better than what would have occurred had they not understood one another's concerns. And there is another possibility. Sometimes it turns out that what appeared to be incompatible aims, though truly different, are not in fact mutually exclusive. A policy might be established that allows both to attain their central purposes.

It is, of course, unlikely that everything for which each side hopes will be attained. That is not the kind of world in which we live. But during the course of dialogue both may become clearer as to what is of *primary* concern to each. Separated from a cluster of secondary concerns, these primary concerns may be quite compatible. A policy may be found which had not been considered by either partner in advance that fulfills the primary concerns of both. This is no longer properly conceived as a compromise. It is a creative advance.

Let us move back to the dialogue between believers of two traditions. Usually there is no need to come to agreement about an action. Hence the partners in dialogue may be satisfied to end with mutual understanding. Often that is thought to be what dialogue is all about, and certainly such dialogue is worthwhile.

But from the Christian side there is an impulse to go on, to go beyond dialogue as thus understood. This impulse comes from a strong Christian sense that in God all things cohere, that there cannot be another truth that is alien to God's truth. Often when the Christian appreciatively understands what the other is saying, and when the effort to interpret that as an already familiar part of Christian belief breaks down, then the Christian wants to see whether this new and different idea can cohere with Christian faith. It is not comfortable to the Christian to recognize that there is a wisdom from which faith shuts one out.

It is at this point that the greatest danger arises. One recognizes that one's faith, a faith that had previously seemed comprehensive and adequate, has left something out. One's initial efforts simply to appropriate this to add it to the existing content of faith, are likely to be unsuccessful. One realizes that one's faith does not have the completeness one had thought, that there are other faiths embodying other strengths. One concludes that the Christian faith is one faith among others. The corrosive acids of relativism begin to do their work.

That there is an alternative to this relativism cannot be assumed *a priori*, but experience in other areas encourages the search. Relativism is like the compromise of the preceding example. It accepts the initial appearance that the needs of the two groups, in this case the beliefs of the two traditions, are essentially incompatible. That this *may* be the case cannot be denied in advance, but even a casual inspection of what occurs in conversation indicates that it is not always the case. Hence, it is a serious mistake to accept incompatibility as final in any given instance without the most intensive efforts to find another solution. The inner impulse of dialogue is to proceed to that point at which the *central* intentions and convictions of both partners can be affirmed without contradiction. That certainly will entail many changes in the beliefs of both. With complete systems it is very unlikely that all that is said in one can be compatible with all that is said in the other. But it is not nearly so unlikely that the deepest insights of each are compatible with one another.

III. Christian assumptions underlying dialogue

There are some deep Christian assumptions at work in shaping this program. There is the assumption that there is a reality distinct from human opinions about it, and that in one way or another human beings are involved with that reality. There is the assumption that patterns of life and thought that are attuned to that reality are better than those that are not – more functional in practice and more satisfying to the mind. Hence there is the assumption that great traditions that have given guidance to people of all types over centuries and millennia, that have produced holy living and shaped durable societies, are not likely to be based on sheer error or illusion. And there is the assumption that what is true in another tradition cannot be incompatible with what is true in one's own.

There is also a long Christian tradition of self-criticism, individual and collective. Christians know of the power of sin to distort thinking as well as action. They know that the faith is given to them in earthen vessels, that every expression is conditioned by time, place, and circumstance, and even by selfish interests. They know that the task of attaining a purer and more adequate formulation of faith is an endless one, that the church is always in need of reformation of both thought and action. In such a context the discovery of difference ceases to be only a threat. It is also an opportunity and a challenge.

The normative Christian program is therefore to go through dialogue beyond dialogue. That is, we begin with the effort to understand. That task is never complete; so we must revert to it again and again. But beyond the accurate grasp of another's thought there is the question of what can be learned from it. In a few cases one may simply add a belief or two to the corpus of already held opinions. But this is rare. Normally what seems worth learning challenges what is currently believed. The task is to refine and hone what one has taken to be important to one's own faith and similarly to refine and hone the insight one is learning from others. The goal is to find how the truth in both coheres.

This is a very different program from another that might be mistaken for it. The Christian might assume that because there is only one reality, the dialogue partner and the Christian must be experiencing the same aspects of that one reality. In that case the range of possible differences is often narrowed to two options. The message of the other may be forced into forms closer to one's own received understanding, or one may change one's own views to adjust to the partner's teaching. The goal in this case is to discover the *identity* of insight underlying diversity of expression.

That sometimes works. It is always possible that the other tradition is dealing with the same aspects of reality as one's own. In that case the discussion is to enrich or purify what one already knows about that aspect of reality from one's own tradition. For example, there can be little doubt that Christianity and Islam are focusing on the same aspect of reality as Judaism. They have learned from Judaism to attend to God. In the dialogue with Islam Christians may learn more about the God they already know in their own faith. They may need to learn to speak of God's acts and characteristics in new ways so as to take account of the experience and insights of Islam.

But when the Christian confronts a tradition that insists it is not attending to God, Christians should listen to that denial. To assume that the partner is wrong, that what is being attended to is after all what Christians already know as God, is likely to mean that they are not truly hearing what is said. Then they impose meaning on the other that prevents them from learning what can be learned. Alternatively, as they hear all the things that are rejected in the other tradition in relation to that to which it does attend, they may be ready, for the sake of agreements, to jettison all those same features in relation to God. Much of great value is thereby lost.

These options arise especially in dialogue with Zen Buddhists. These Buddhists point to Emptiness or Emptying instead of to God. What does that mean? To those who assume that all traditions must be focusing on the same aspects of reality, it means that Emptying must be the same as God. Then either one must interpret what the Zen Buddhist is saying about Emptying in a way that moderates its full radicality, or one must employ the negative theology on the Christian heritage so radically as to dissolve God into Emptying. In that process everything distinctive of the biblical heritage is lost. In comparison to this, a relativism that abandons the effort to correlate the beliefs of the two traditions is an inviting alternative.

But if instead the foci of the two traditions are seen as compatible without being identical, a richer option presents itself. Surely the Zen Buddhists cannot be fundamentally mistaken about Emptying. What they say grows too closely out of actual experience, experience that is humanly transforming in ways Christians must admire, to be basically erroneous. As the Zen Buddhists would be the first to say, this does not guarantee the exact accuracy of every verbal formulation. Far from it. These are intended only as pointers toward the insight itself or as guides toward its practical realization.

On the other side, the Christian cannot believe that the whole scriptural witness rests on fundamental error and illusion. That does not mean that within this rich and complex tradition, everything that is said is fully consistent or credible. Much of it is not intended straightforwardly, for the biblical word, too, points to a reality to which it is inadequate. But what it points to is not what the Zen Buddhists point to: Emptying as such.

Is it not conceivable that in the full complexity of reality, so far exceeding all that we can know or think, "Emptying" identifies one truly important aspect, and "God" another? I think so: Would acknowledging that possibility contradict fundamentally what it is most important to either Zen Buddhists or Christians to assert? I think not. But to come to that conclusion does require that one rethink the insights on both sides.

This is not the place to carry through that work. I have tried to do so elsewhere. Here, the concern is simply to indicate different lines of thought to which dialogue can lead us that do not result in relativism. They result instead in the purification of our own faith and the enrichment of our comprehensive vision. The process is never complete, but it is a healthy one.

IV. Faith and dialogue

This process of purification and enrichment is also the one that most fully expresses and embodies faith itself. Faith is not a particular set of beliefs. It may be understood in many ways, but central to all of them is trust. Trust is directed to Jesus, to the living Christ, to the Holy Spirit. Fundamentally we trust in God. We trust God to forgive us our sins. We trust God also for the needs of daily life. We also trust that when we are truly open, when we surrender our defensiveness, when we allow the distortions of self-interest and fear to be set aside, we are led into deeper truth. The fullness of truth comes at the end. Now we see through a glass darkly. We must not absolutize what we now see for the sake of worldly security. We must be open to its change and transformation as we are led by the Holy Spirit into new truth. Faith involves all of that. It cannot be clinging to the familiar, however comfortable that is.

This certainly does not mean that faith is chasing after every ephemeral novelty in search of kicks. It does not mean that any of the deeply held convictions shaped by past Christian experience and reflection will be lightly set aside. It does not mean rebelliousness against the authority of the church. It does not mean casual criticism of the Bible. It does not mean relativism.

Faith will express itself in the struggle to integrate new experience, new insights, with old ones. In this process nothing remains quite the same. This is the process of maturing in faith that goes on quite apart from the encounter with other faiths. The encounter with other faiths extends and enlarges the maturing process. Much that was unchallenged and hence unreflected while we remained listening only to those who shared our tradition becomes problematic when we hear the words of those who come from other traditions. We cannot set the limits of the growth and change which that will bring about. To try to do so expresses lack of trust in God.

For many Christians these are hard words to hear. Faith is understood to mean belief that certain ideas are true or it is so bound up with such ideas that if they are surrendered faith itself crumbles. There is truth in this. There is no faith that is separable from the matrix of beliefs. For example, faith becomes meaningless if one comes to the conclusion that nothing is worthy of trust. It would be pointless to call faith Christian if one did not believe that Christ is bound up with that which is worthy of trust. Does that mean that there are some beliefs that must be established and held to regardless of evidence and argument? Does it mean that we should avoid listening to those who might challenge these beliefs?

The situation may seem paradoxical. We begin by trusting God as we know and experience God in Christ. We find that to trust God means that we are open to hearing and learning whatever is to be heard or learned. But we are told there is a danger, that perhaps what we learn will lead us to deny that there is a trustworthy God. To me it seems that those who warn of this danger are lacking in faith in the trustworthy God. They seem to think that if we are open to hearing the truth we will discover that there is nothing to trust. To whatever extent we truly believe there is a trustworthy God, to whatever extent we have faith, we will have confidence that we can be open to all truth, that the openness to truth will strengthen our faith.

Does that mean that we should set these doctrines aside as beyond discussion in dialogue or beyond transformation through dialogue? To do that would be an act of un-faith; it would imply that the faith that opens us to the other is not justified by reality, so that it must be protected against the consequences of that openness.

No human being can know what will happen to her or to him in the course of time. I who now believe may cease to believe. No defensive wall built around my present opinions will assure that they will continue! Indeed, testifying to their insecurity by trying to protect my beliefs makes it more likely that in my heart of hearts I will cease to believe. How widespread for how long have been recitations of beliefs in which we have vested little existential confidence! A faith that protects itself from risk, even the risk that it will cease to exist, is not the total faith to which Christians are called.

V. Dialogue, persuasion, and conversion

Often, for the sake of dialogue, a sharp distinction is made between dialogue and evangelistic witness. The latter aims at conversion, the former does not. Such a distinction can be justified, and as a practical matter it may be important in order to assure the dialogue partners that the invitation to dialogue is not a trick. Proponents of other faiths are so accustomed to a Christian proclamation that simply confronts them that they must be assured that the intention of dialogue is not simply to provide a new context for such a confrontation.

Nevertheless, the sharp distinction is misleading. It applies to the initial stage of dialogue where the focus of attention is mutual understanding and mutual appreciation. But even there an element of confrontation can be found. As Christians listen to others interpreting back what they have heard, Christians may sense a stubborn refusal to hear. Confrontation may be the only way to get attention to the point being made. Still, the purpose of such confrontation is to serve the cause of genuine understanding, not conversion.

When dialogue moves beyond an exchange of views to mutual critique the confrontative element becomes larger and the distinction from evangelistic witness declines. Christians confront their dialogue partners with the limitations of their views when these are seen in Christian perspective, with perceived inconsistencies, or with what are from the Christian point of view dangerous consequences implicit in what they affirm. Even if this confrontation is primarily in the service of clearer understanding, it is also for the sake of persuasion. The Christian wants to persuade the dialogue partner that change is needed.

Dialogue is not in contradiction to persuasion. On the contrary. When dialogue is truly free, Christians will affirm their own convictions passionately. And those convictions normally include the view that their partners in dialogue should share these convictions. Christians will be as persuasive as they can. Christians also listen to what their partners say, and they want their partners to be as persuasive as possible in the way they present their beliefs. It is only thus that Christians can gain the most from the interchange. Real dialogue consists in the effort of both sides to persuade the other.

Furthermore, persuasion is more likely to succeed in the context of dialogue than in sheer confrontation. When one is confronted with strange ideas and asked to give up one's own inherited wisdom in exchange for them, there is natural and healthy resistance. Why should one reject the wisdom one has for barely understood new ideas that have not been tested in the context of one's own life or cultural tradition? Especially if the confrontation shows lack of understanding of what one is and believes, it is quite easy to dismiss it as ignorant and misdirected. But when the new ideas come in the context of dialogue, when the one who proposes them understands one's own ideas quite well and formulates the new ideas in their relevance to the old, then it is much harder to dismiss them. In this sense dialogue is the ideal context for evangelistic witness, not its opposite.

On the other hand, there does remain a difference. Usually evangelistic witness is understood to aim at conversion. It aims to draw people out of the religious communities in which they have lived and into the community of the Christian church. It ignores the wisdom of the other community and hence implies that this wisdom should be set aside in favor of Christian truth. It thus aims to supersede the other tradition. When it is completely successful, the other tradition may disappear altogether, along with its insights and special disciplines.

Dialogue, in contrast, assumes that there are values in the other tradition, that its obliteration would be a loss rather than a gain. It aims more to persuade persons in the other tradition of the truth of Christian faith than to draw them out of their own communities and into the Christian church. The transformation of the other traditions ranks higher as a goal than their supersession. To whatever extent the word conversion is bound up with the abandonment by converts of other traditions and the communities in which they live, then it is not a good word for the goal of Christians in dialogue. Instead, we may say that in dialogue, and beyond dialogue, Christians seek to be transformed and to transform others through mutual witness.

VI. Exclusive claims and dialogue

Whereas some Christians fear dialogue because they suppose it endangers faith, others oppose it because it seems to reject from the start the radical claims to the unique and exclusive work of Jesus Christ. It seems to assume, in this respect at least, a certain relativism. To see the other tradition as worthy to be a dialogue partner is to accord it rough parity. But is it not at the heart of Christianity to claim that it is the only way to salvation? If so, do Christians not betray their tradition in the act that respects another as comparable in worth?

There is no doubt but that the dialogical approach communicates in its very nature, regardless of what is said, a respect for religious traditions other than Christianity. It sets aside, at least provisionally, the questions of ranking these traditions as better or worse. It certainly sets aside all claims of an exclusiveness that entails a monopoly of wisdom. Is that in contradiction to Christian belief?

Surely not if the issue is one between institutions or historical communities! Christians know that they as human beings along with their human institutions are fallible and ignorant. They can learn from many sources. Their whole history is one of such learning when new information is not stubbornly refused. As human beings none would question that they can learn from Buddhists or Muslims.

But Christians have been accustomed to pointing beyond themselves to Christ. In Christ, they have believed, is the fullness of truth and grace. Christ is the Way and the Life. Only in Christ has God been present reconciling the world. There is no salvation in any other name. It is the apparent surrender of these bold claims that causes deep uneasiness. Do Christians abandon these beliefs when they sit down for dialogue with Jews or Hindus? There are several levels of response to this important question.

First, not all claims to exclusive supremacy are meant as objectively literal statements. A woman who says she has the best mother in the world is saying more about her feelings about the mother than about the exact comparative merits of her mother and all others. If a patriotic Englishman announces that his is the best of all nations, and a patriotic Frenchman makes the same claim about his, the initial reaction would be to be impressed with their fervor and devotion, not to ask for objective evidence.

But let us pursue the second example further. Suppose, somewhat to our surprise, the response of each was to insist that he did mean quite objectively exactly what he said and that he was prepared to debate the matter with any who disputed his claim. What would happen? We would expect from each a recital of the great achievements of his nation and its outstanding qualities. We would expect the lists to be different. The greatness of France might be demonstrated by the excellence of its cuisine, that of England, by the efficiency of its public servants. Let us suppose, in order to get on with the example, that each could prove the superiority of his nation in terms of the area he chose. That would leave open the question of the relative importance of cuisine and bureaucracy. The Frenchman might argue strongly that cuisine is more important as a measure of national greatness; the Englishman would argue for bureaucracy. But would this not cease to be a worthwhile discussion? If the respective greatness of the two nations is to be seriously debated, then a clear definition of greatness must come first. Yet it is unlikely that agreement could be found on such a definition which would, by specifying the areas relevant to the discussion, largely predetermine the outcome. There is likely to be a circular relationship between what Englishmen care most about and what they excel in, and so also for the French.

The relation among religious traditions is similar. In terms of what Hindus care most about, it is unlikely that they are excelled by Muslims. But in terms of what Muslims care most about, it is unlikely that they are excelled by Hindus. Since Muslims attribute what they find of supreme importance to Allah and his prophet, they will make strong claims for the unique and decisive importance of Allah and Mohammed. Since Vedantist Hindus attribute all that is most important to them to the orientation of all life and culture to Brahman and the realization of the identity of Atman and Brahman, they will make strong statements about what is ultimate. Does the truth of one claim exclude that of the other?

It can. Go back to the earlier example. The Frenchman may be convinced that the Englishman is simply wrong in attributing so much importance to bureaucracy. For him, part of the inferiority of England consists in its misdirection of its interests. For its own sake England should concentrate on cuisine and learn from the French. Then Englishmen would see that all along the French had been correct about their superiority.

Both Muslims and Hindus are likely to make these types of judgments as well. These judgments make dialogue difficult. The act of dialogue involves a provisional bracketing of judgments at this level. Muslims will not cease to believe that what Allah and Mohammed have done for Muslims is of greater importance than what Hindus have attained through their under-standing of Brahman. But they will adopt an attitude of openness to the theoretical possibility that what Hindus have learned and experienced is of comparable interest and importance. They will listen to what that is and to why it seems so valuable to Hindus. They will in principle acknowledge that not only can they thereby get more information about Hindus but that they may learn something of interest and value to themselves. In this sense they give up their exclusivist claims.

But does this mean that they start out by giving up the belief that there is only one God, Allah, and that Mohammed is his prophet? Surely not! If they did, there would be nothing to dialogue about. They enter the dialogue precisely to explain what that means and how it is experienced as of supreme importance to them, and they hope that when their dialogue partners really hear this truth they will be persuaded. Muslims will not try to decide in advance what aspects of the Vedantists' beliefs will have to be rejected or changed in order for this truth to be appropriated. If they are willing to enter dialogue at all, that means that they allow a certain autonomy for Hindus to participate in making judgments about the implications of what they are learning from Muslims.

VII. Salvation and dialogue

But does not the situation change when the Christian makes the claim that only in Jesus Christ can any human being find salvation? In this case the argument does not seem to be about the respective merits of two systems of life, thought, and religious practice. It is about salvation itself. And that seems to transcend all the rest.

Does it? That deserves more careful attention. If a woman who knows her sins forgiven through Jesus Christ cries out that he and none other is the savior, that is not initially and primarily to be understood as an objective claim about what has gone on thousands of years in the past or in remote parts of the world. She may have sought help fruitlessly in many quarters. Now she has found it through Jesus. He is her Lord and Savior – none other. The cry is authentic, existential, and doxological. Most of the church's initial pronouncements on this subject had this character. Later, as these pronouncements became doctrines, and as these doctrines in turn became starting points for drawing conclusions, the church felt it necessary to make many interesting qualifications. Those who came before Jesus could be saved by anticipating him. Those who did not have the chance to respond to the message, waited in limbo for him to come and preach to them. Righteous people who did not have the chance to hear the message could be saved by implicit faith. A baptized baby could be saved quite apart from believing in Jesus. And so it goes and has always gone, while alongside this softening, there have been those who clung to the unqualified assertion, accepting all its stark and horrible implications.

Even if we give up all the qualifications and translate the doxological utterance into objective historical truth, there remain uncertainties as to its meaning. There was a time when salvation might, for some, mean quite simply going to heaven when we died. Heaven and hell were seen as two objectively distinct realms such that each deceased soul or resurrected body would be in one or the other. In the context of that kind of thinking the issues were, indeed, quite objective. If no one could avoid everlasting hellfire and damnation except through conscious faith in Jesus Christ, then to sit down for dialogue with one who refused that faith might well be implying what was not so. It might be implying that the worldly or mystical wisdom the other might impart was somehow on the same level as the message about how to avoid everlasting torment. Such miscommunication could be thought to prevent the other from taking the one step needful.

For those who understand heaven and hell quite literally and who understand that apart from explicit acknowledgment of faith in Jesus Christ everyone is destined to spend eternity in hell, dialogue is not likely to figure prominently. If they enter dialogue at all, it will be to gain an understanding that may make them more effective evangelists. To those settled in that kind of faith I have little to say. I am ready to dialogue with them, but this is not the place for that.

But for those who relax these highly objectivist views, who understand salvation as something we participate in here and now rather than, or in addition to, life beyond, then there is much to be said. Salvation will for them identify what is most precious and supremely valuable in human life here and now or that for which they most deeply hope. But *that* is not likely to be exactly what is most appreciated and hoped for by Muslims or Hindus. The discussion between Christians and Muslims or Hindus will not be unlike that I have described between Muslims and Hindus. Christians will enter the dialogue convinced that what Christ has to offer, what can come into being in human life only through faith in Christ, is supremely important not only for Christians but for all people. But they will know that Muslims and Hindus do not see things just that way. Provisionally Christians will acknowledge that there may be other ways of thinking, other modes of experience that have supreme value to other communities. An exchange of understanding and experience will be enriching.

For example, suppose that some Christians understand by salvation primarily justification and sanctification interpreted as the forgiveness of sins and liberation from the control of sin over motive and action. These Christians may affirm strongly that this can take place only through faith in Jesus Christ. Suppose now that a Vedantist Hindu asserts that *moksha* can occur only through certain yogic practices. Is there a contradiction? Surely not. Both may be correct. The difference is that the Christian believes that the forgiveness of sins is supremely important, while the Hindu believes that liberation from illusion is supremely important. If the question of what is supremely important is taken to be an objective one, then there is a real debate. But how difficult it is to engage that debate! And how unnecessary! On the other hand, through dialogue Hindus may come to appreciate the importance of sin in human life and the urgency of finding forgiveness. For this they may turn to Jesus Christ. And Christians may in their turn realize how deeply we are all mired in illusions, how they distort all our thinking, and how valid and valuable it is to realize that they are just that, illusions. Christians may adopt yogic practices to help them attain that realization. These things happen. Christians may continue to believe that the forgiveness of sins is more fundamental than what can be attained through yogic practice. Hindus may think that the forgiveness of sins occurs at a level that is finally transcended. If so, the Christians remain Christian and the Hindus Hindu. Each has been transformed through the dialogue, but neither has surrendered the unique universal claims of their traditions.

VIII. Incarnation and dialogue

An objector could reply that even if it were true that at a functional level the effects of Jesus Christ in human history and those of yogic practice can both be affirmed without contradiction, the heart of the Christian claim has to do with the person of Jesus himself. The Christian claim is that in Jesus God became man. This is formulated quite exclusively. This incarnation is not one among many but the one and only such event.

Once again a certain discretion is in order. The affirmations of metaphysical uniqueness of Jesus grew out of doxological statements that did not envision this metaphysical conceptuality or its implications. There is a considerable move from the doxological utterance placed on the lips of Thomas, "My Lord and my God," to the full creedal formulations.

Furthermore, even the creeds do not say quite what they are often taken to say. They attempt to hold to the full humanity of Jesus in a way that many of their interpreters have denied. The problem of just how to understand the real presence of God in this fully human being is certainly a difficult one, and the Christian tendency has been to stress that the way God was present in Jesus has no analogue in any other person. But the denial of such analogues is not at the heart of Thomas' cry, nor even of the Chalcedonian creed. Some interpreters have seen Jesus as the one in whom there is a fullness of a type of presence of God that is known by all believers as grace.

But let us take even the hardest line. Suppose the incarnation of God in Jesus has no analogue whatever, does that prevent openness to what the Hindu has to teach us about liberation from illusion? Why should it? And on the other side, would it prevent a Hindu from appropriating the Christian message? The Hindu has no trouble with incarnations and may be able to allow for one that is quite unique.

The point of all this is to say again that in dialogue with persons of other religious traditions, if the traditions are sufficiently different, the likelihood of flat contradictions is remote. The points that are made are likely to be very different, based on attention to quite different problems and their quite different solutions. But there is no contradiction in the claim of one that problem A is solved by X and the claim of the other that problem B is solved by Y. Both claims may be quite exclusive without arousing conflict. The claims are complementary rather than contradictory. In a larger context than either partner brings initially to the discussion, both can believe both claims. The issue is then one of their respective importance. Judgments on this question give differing shapes to the life of the two communities. If a further step is taken; if, for example, Vedantists are persuaded that after all the forgiveness of sins is more fundamental to human existence than liberation from illusion; then they will, in a very important sense, have been converted, whether or not they join a Christian church. And, of course, vice versa.

IX. Christian-Jewish dialogue

Flat contradictions arise much more when the dialogue partners come from closely related traditions. Between Buddhists and Hindus there may be real contradictions. This is a difficult question. Most Buddhists think so, most Hindus do not. It is a topic on which dialogue should continue.

Also, between Christians and Jews there have seemed to be such contradictions. In the early church the Christians said that Jesus was the Messiah, the Jews denied it. If a contradiction was not involved, that could only be because there was a shift of meaning in the word "Messiah." Actually there was. The Christians acknowledged that Jesus had not brought in the Messianic age but held that he would return and do so. Hence for Jesus to be the Messiah meant, in Jewish terms, that he was the one who would in the future be the Messiah. Yet since the Jews who did not become Christians did not believe that there would be this connection between Jesus and the future Messiah, there remained a contradiction.

Rather rapidly, however, the identification of Jesus with the Jewish Messiah became less prominent and less essential for Christians. Jesus was seen instead as the incarnate Word, for example. That was quite different from what "Messiah" meant to Jews. There were many opportunities to overcome the flat contradiction between Jewish and Christian assertions, but the mood in the early church was quite different. It was to establish itself over against the Jews. The anti-Jewish polemic was sustained, bitter, and destructive.

The question is now, when we do seek dialogue, whether our christological claims lead to flat contradictions. In their harshest, most literal forms, they do. Since Jews, like Christians, are interested in the forgiveness of sins, and since what they mean by this is quite similar, the exclusive claim objectively made that no one's sins have ever been forgiven who has not explicitly acknowledged Jesus as personal savior flatly contradicts Jewish beliefs. Yet such strong claims have been rare in Christianity. It is usually believed that God had a covenantal relationship with Jews that dealt with the question of sin and salvation. The debate is not about absolute possibilities but about whether the establishment of a new covenant through Jesus invalidated the old, made it of no effect. That is a topic on which contemporary dialogue has been useful.

Many Christians find that they can make strong statements about the importance, the necessity for them and for Gentiles generally, of the new covenant in Jesus Christ without proceeding to the negative statement that God abolished the covenants he had made with Abraham and Moses. What is gained in making such negative statements? If these negations are avoided and rejected, then much of the Christian claim ceases to contradict the Jewish one. Once the contradiction is removed, Christians and Jews can learn from one another quite freely. Now that Pope John Paul II has called God's covenant with the Jews irrevocable and major Protestant denominations have repudiated the idea that the Christian covenant supersedes the Jewish one, the approach I suggest is hardly radical.

It had long been thought that the Christian claim that made this mutual openness most difficult was that of the resurrection of Jesus. That seemed to give divine sanction to the Christian claim to have superseded Judaism. Recently, however, it has become very clear that this is not so. An orthodox Jewish Rabbi, Pinchas Lapide, has stated unequivocally that there is nothing in his faith that requires him to deny the most literal and supernatural view of the resurrection of Jesus. In his view God intervened supernaturally so that the salvation already known by the Jews could be carried to the Gentiles as well. The resurrection of Jesus is, in his view, of little importance to Jews so far as their own covenant with God is concerned. But it is of supreme importance to the Gentiles. Need a Christian disagree?

X. Understanding an exclusivist text

By itself, the fact that apparent contradictions can usually be resolved into non-contradictory differences is important. It opens up a new day in the relation among the world's great traditions. But by itself, that does not alter the way most of the believers in each tradition think. The change of attitude at the popular level is of great importance for the future of the world. Here each community must find its own way ahead.

For Christians the central task is to understand the biblical texts in fresh ways. I will conclude my essay with a single example, a text often used to emphasize the exclusiveness of Jesus against all others: "I am the way, the truth, and the life. No one comes to the Father but by me" (John 14:6). What does that really mean? And can we believe what it really means without entailing the pejorative implications for Jews and others that have so often been drawn from it?

Of course, sophisticated Christians have long learned to distance themselves from texts whose message offends them. Jefferson led the way with scissors and paste, selecting what he could affirm in the Bible and rejecting the rest. But we know that does not work. The selective process is inevitable, but the passages that do not speak to one generation are often just those that speak to another. We cannot simply dismiss this verse and others like it. We must consider them all seriously.

To begin, let us ask, who is the "I" who speaks? It is, of course, the Johannine Jesus. Now it lies open to all to see that the Johannine Jesus does not speak in the same way as the Jesus of the synoptic gospels. If our interest is with the historical Jesus, we must turn to the latter and work through layers of tradition to find the authentic sayings. That is irrelevant in John. The Jesus of John is the Jesus of faith, the Jesus of the imagination of the early church, shaped of course by memories of historical events but more by the living experience of Christ in the community.

The structure of the gospel makes this clear. There is no story of Jesus' birth. There is rather the incarnation of the Word. The one who came into the world was the Word that had been with God from the beginning, the Word that was God. It is this Word that speaks as "I" in the pages of the gospel.

It is affirmed, then, that the Word who is incarnate in Jesus is the Way, the Truth, the Life, and that no one comes to the Father except through that Word. This cannot mean that the Word is present and active *only* in Jesus; for in the prologue to the Gospel it is stated that in the Word that was from the beginning was life, that this life was also the true light that enlightens everyone.

There is here, too, an exclusive claim. It is that the presence of the everlasting Word, which was with God from the beginning, which, indeed, *is* God, is the one and only source of life and human understanding. This means that finally every effort to explain life and human understanding apart from God will be incomplete. But this exclusivist claim does not exclude from relevance and truth what chemists and biologists can tell us about life or what physiologists and psychologists can tell us about human understanding.

The claim has an exclusivist element as it is addressed to Hindus and Buddhists. We claim as Christians to know the source of their life and understanding also. That source is the everlasting Word that was incarnate in Jesus. But this does not invalidate their understanding and wisdom. Far from. it! On the other hand, it may complement it by calling their attention to its deeper source – a source some of them have neglected and even denied.

In relation to Jews the identification of the everlasting Word as the Way, the Truth, and the Life need not be a source of tension. Jews resist the trinitarian formulations to which reflection on the Word and the Father gave rise in Christianity. But that the Word of God has worked creatively and redemptively from the beginning is no surprise to them.

The break with Judaism comes when we are told that this Word became flesh and dwelt among us in a single human being. The idea of the Word becoming flesh is not Jewish, and as it worked itself out in the metaphysical doctrines of incarnation, it became increasingly alien. Jews saw God's presence more in the people as a whole than in individuals. Still, there is no contradiction here, however deep the difference. Christians need not deny the covenant relationship of the Jewish people to God in order to affirm the incarnation of the Word in Jesus. Whatever the author of the Gospel of John may have thought or meant in the heat of controversy, the Jewish covenant also embodied the Way, the Truth, and the Life that led to the Father.

Christians may well believe that through the historically incarnate Word they grasp, or are grasped by, the truth of the everlasting and universal Word with unique fullness. That is a legitimate starting point for dialogue. Unique fullness in Jesus does not predetermine what knowledge of the Word is to be found elsewhere, whether it will only reinforce parts of what is known or will also supplement the knowledge Christians have been vouchsafed.

A different issue arises in relation to traditions that do not deal thematically with the source of life and human understanding that John 14:6 declares to be the Way, the Truth, and the Life. According to what is said here, these traditions cannot lead people to the Father. In terms of Christian goals this is a devastating limitation. To be denied access to God the Father is to be missing what is most important.

But we have seen in earlier discussions that what is supremely important in one tradition is not always of great importance in others. The Vedantist Hindus and Zen Buddhists do not agree that coming to the Father is of supreme importance. They could agree that it is the Word that leads to the Father, while not supposing that the Word is of crucial importance. For them the realization of Atman as Brahman, or of Emptying, is of much greater importance. We are back to the issue of importance with which we have dealt above.

To whatever extent John 14:6 had its locus in the anti-Jewish polemic of the early church, the task today is to differentiate our use of the verse from the original one. To do this does not require a repudiation of the verse or of its central meaning. On the contrary, this verse can function as a summation of the heart of the Christian claim. The point of this discussion is that the heart of the Christian claim does not contradict the core affirmations of other traditions. In the course of dialogue that can be made clear by honing our formulations and theirs as well. Through that process we will all be purified and enriched.

Interreligious Dialogue: What? Why? How?

—

Paul F. Knitter

From my own experience – gained in conference rooms, libraries, and meditation halls – I would describe interreligious dialogue as the confrontation with utter, bewildering, often threatening *differences* and at the same time, the *trust* that such differences are, for the most part, friendly rather than hostile, fruitful rather than barren. In dialogue one faces the utterly other and trusts that one can speak to, learn from, even work with that other. Within the heart of dialogue, therefore, there beats a deep act of faith and trust.

Unpacking this description, I find four pivotal elements in dialogue: 1. the experience of *difference*; 2. the *trust* that such differences are unitive rather than separative; and flowing from these two experiences, 3. the resolve to *witness*, that is, to make known to one's dialogical partner one's own religious experiences and convictions; 4. and the resolve to *listen and learn* from the experiences and convictions of one's partner. As part of my efforts to state what for me constitutes the nature and goals of dialogue, I will try to explore the meaning and demands of these four ingredients. Then I'd like to state why I think that the present state of our suffering and liberation-needy world is providing all religious believers with a newly felt *imperative* and *opportunity* to mix those ingredients and pursue interreligious dialogue. Responding to this new imperative and opportunity, I would then like to suggest a liberation-centred (or "soteriocentric") model for interreligious dialogue which, I think, will both make for a more effective encounter of religions and will enable Christians to remove one of their main stumbling blocks to dialogue – their traditional understanding of the exclusivity or superiority of Christ and Christianity. All this makes for the what, the why, and the how of dialogue.

Dialogue: what is it?

Differences

Anyone who begins an interreligious conversation with the announcement of how much we have in common or that we are really saying "the same thing in different words" has done just that – only begun the conversation. Such announcements, though they may have their element of truth, can be maintained only on the surface of dialogue; they begin to fade away as one goes deeper into the experience, the beliefs and practices, and the historical development of the different religious traditions. Like a newly married couple growing out of the first stages of infatuation into real living together, partners in religious sharing, as they get to know each other, soon arrive at the existential realization of how bewilderingly different they are. What had been initially experienced as similarities now become differing, even opposing, faces. The Tao and God, Zen meditation and Christian prayer, Jesus and Buddha, *avidya* and original sin – become as different as they once were similar. One gradually becomes aware of the naiveté and the downright danger of proclaiming a "common essence" or a "common core" within all the religions of the world. Yes, one might still believe that Ultimate Reality or God is one and that ultimately differences will be swallowed in oneness; but right now, in the dust and dirt of the real world, we have to deal with the manyness, the differences, among the religions before we can ever contemplate, much less realize, their possible unity or oneness.

In reflecting on this experience of difference, I find myself in basic agreement with the so-called "anti-foundationalists." Today, philosophers such as Richard Rorty and Richard Bernstein, together with theologians such as George Lindbeck, Francis Schüssler Fiorenza, David Tracy, and Raimundo Panikkar chide religious dialoguers who are looking for a common "religious esperanto" or are proposing a "universal theology of religions" (Swidler 1987) or a "world theology" (Smith 1981) that they may be searching for a chimera or imposing an ideological system (Panikkar 1987a, 1987b). As far as we can tell, in this finite world of many cultures and religions and histories, there is no universal foundation outside the fray of history and diversity on which we can make universal judgments and assess the diversity. Plurality is it! It will not yield an Archimedean point by which we can lift ourselves beyond the plurality to a final unity. Or so it seems.

We are, in a sense, caught in our own cultural-religious perspectives – or at least inescapably influenced by them. If there is no such thing as "pure experience;" if all experience is "interpreted," then we are always looking at the world through our inherited cultural-religious spectacles (Katz 1978, 26). As Lindbeck convincingly points out, we don't first have an experience of God or of ultimacy and then turn to our religion to "interpret" or "represent" it; rather, our religion's interpretation or language has a determinative influence on what kind of religious experience we have (Lindbeck 1985, 40, 49). If the interpretations are markedly different ("Emptiness" vs. "God"), then the experiences will be equally different.

Between the religions of the world, therefore, there yawn "incommensurability gaps" – even between their mystics (Katz 1982)! We can look at and speak to one another, we can form some "picture" of who the other is, but we cannot really understand one another sufficiently to pass judgments on the truth or falsity, the goodness or harmfulness, of one another's religious beliefs and practices. That would require moving beyond our own historico-cultural perspectives or limitations and taking on, thoroughly, that of the others. But that is extremely difficult, if not impossible. Since there seems to be no universal "foundation" beyond our particular "standpoints," every time we judge another's religion we are doing so from our own "standpoint," not theirs. We are doing so from outside their religion. And that's not fair.

Given my own experience of dialogue and thanks to the chidings of my anti-foundationalist friends, I have realized over the past years that I, like many proponents of religious pluralism, have too hastily hoisted the banner of "pluralism," before sufficiently recognizing the reality of "plurality." We pluralists have been too quick to propose an "ism" or a system on the vast, buzzing array of plurality; and in so *proposing* we have *imposed*. David Tracy's admonition, arising out of his own experience of religious otherness, rings true:

> ... the official pluralist too often finds ways to reduce real otherness and genuine differences to some homogenized sense of what we (who is this "we"?) already know ... some pluralists, the vaunted defenders of difference, can become the great reductionists – reducing differences to mere similarity, reducing otherness to the same, and reducing plurality to my community of right-thinking competent critics. In this light, there is truth in Simone de Beauvoir's bitter charge that "pluralism is the perfect ideology for the bourgeois mind" (Tracy 1987b, 12).

Trust

And yet, though we stare at each others' religious traditions across these incommensurability gaps, though we well realize the difficulty of understanding, and the danger of judging, another person's religious beliefs and practices, we find ourselves borne or grasped by a suspicion, a hope, a resolve that we *can* speak to each other across our religious barriers; that it is worthwhile, even necessary, to do so. This is, indeed, an act of faith. It is a deep-seated feeling which seems to be given to us or to take hold of us; we find ourselves believing in something which, though rooted in experiential evidence, goes beyond that evidence. It is similar to Luther's "*trotzdem,*" his "despite all that:" despite the stark differences between religions, we believe

that the sheer actuality of *plurality* can lead to the inter-relatedness of
pluralism. There is *life* in the differences. In speaking to one another across
our gaps, we can come closer.

In fact, it seems that this coming closer, this conversation with those who
are genuinely different, is an indispensable condition for growing in the
understanding of reality, in the pursuit of truth. If there is no absolute
criterion of truth given to us from above, if there is no foundation outside the
waves of history for evaluating the many forced opinions that face our world,
then we must plunge into the conversation, listen to each others' differences,
and in this engagement fashion, step by difficult step, our understanding of
reality. In order to "grow in wisdom and truth before God and our fellow
human beings," we must talk to each other. In order to enrich and save our
world we must embrace pluralism. ". . . Pluralism is a responsible and
fruitful option because it allows for (indeed demands) that we develop better
ways as selves, as communities of inquirers, as societies, as cultures, as an
inchoately global culture to allow for more possibilities to enrich our personal
and communal lives" (Tracy 1987b, 9).

In the ebb and flow of conversing, with all its complexity and dangers, we
can create, not foundations, but "shaky common ground." Not with pre-
packaged methods or systems but by genuinely trying to "pass over" to the
otherness of the other, by stretching our own visions and paradigms, we can
establish new, shared ground on which we *can* truly understand another
culture or religion, and they us. The gap of incommensurability *can* be
bridged – but the bridge will never be set in cement; it will, rather, sway in the
wind and have to be frequently reconstructed or torn down to be rebuilt at a
better crossing. Just how these bridges are built and how this common shaky
ground is discovered cannot be stated in advance of the conversation. It can
be discovered, created, maintained only in the act and process of dialogue.

Witnessing

In interreligious dialogue we confront otherness as something we want not
only to embrace but also to address. Ideally, we come to the conversation
from a position of richness, not impoverishment – that is, we speak to each
other out of our own religious experience. We speak because we have
discovered something of value – the pearl of great price. As Raimundo
Panikkar has continuously insisted, in order to have religious encounter, we
must speak from religious experience – or at least from religious quest. Such
"subjective" contents and perspectives are not to be cut out and packed in
some kind of deep-freeze "epoché" but, rather, are to be poured, warm and
bubbling, into the conversation (Panikkar 1978). The "object" of dialogue is
approached through a meeting of "subjects."

And because we speak out of our different religious experiences and
convictions, we will seek not only to explain but to *persuade*. If genuinely
experienced, religious truth, like all truth, can never be only "for me." If it is,

it is somehow diluted or not yet fully grown. A quality of "universal relevance" is ingredient to every encounter with or revelation of the Ultimate; what one has seen, felt, been transformed by – can also so affect others. All interreligious dialogue, therefore, is animated by a certain missionary élan. We want our partners to see what we have seen; we want their lives to be touched and transformed as ours have been. Yes, let me use the offensive word: we want to *convert* our partners.

But the conversion that is sought is not one of "winning over" but of sharing. This is a big difference – between saving from damnation and sharing the light. This distinction is based on the difference between religious truth experienced as "universally relevant" and as "one and only." Authentic religious experience naturally includes the former quality, not the latter. When experienced, truth is always felt to be *universal*; it is not necessarily felt to be *singular* or *final*. In Christian terms, the God who has spoken *for all peoples* in Jesus Christ has not necessarily spoken *only* in Jesus Christ. Therefore, what animates me in the dialogue is not the conviction that you are lost without my understanding of truth, but that there *is* something missing in your life until you have seen what I have seen. You can be different, richer, if I can pass on to you what has been passed on to me.

All this paints a rather idealistic picture of the element of witnessing in dialogue. Witnessing can take in other forms, and be present in different degrees. We might enter the dialogue not from a position of strength but from one of weakness; or better, a position of searching rather than of discovery; perhaps it is a position of dissatisfaction with one's own tradition. While genuine conversation can arise from such states of dissatisfaction or insecurity, I would not spotlight them as the ideal, as does Peter Berger when he urges that the most profitable kind of religious dialogue is that "between people who are very unsure of their position rather than people who are firmly committed to their traditions" (1981, 36). Also, in holding that we give witness in order to "enrich" not to "save," I don't want to rule out the demands of situations in which we confront what we feel is genuine *evil* in the other's attitude or practices; then the conversion we seek is much more a matter of *metanoia*, of trying to "turn around" our partners, rather than of clarifying or enhancing what they already know. Or, as the liberation theologians would put it, announcing often requires denouncing.

Learning

But the dialectical pendulum swings back, and just as much as we desire to witness and convert, we feel the need to be witnessed to and, yes, converted by our partners. Witnessing will go astray unless it is accompanied by listening and learning. This need to learn from others is rooted in the same "trust," described above, that the "other" has words of life to speak to us. But it is also rooted in and demanded by our own religious experience. In Christian terms, to experience the living God is not only to experience a truth and a power that is "universally relevant," to be proclaimed to all the nations; it is also to fall into the embrace of a Mystery that will always and enticingly be more than what we have experienced. To experience this Mystery of God authentically is to know for sure that we are experiencing it only *partially*. All religious traditions seem to bear witness to this aspect of religious experience – that God, Allah, Brahman, Sunyata, the Tao – can never be known *in toto* but only *in parte*. And if only partially, then we must be open to discovering "other parts;" we must look through other windows out on to the universe of Truth and Mystery. As wonderful as is the view from our window, it impels us to look through others. Max Müller's worn dictum holds true: "Those who know one, know none."

The need to learn from others is also fostered by what cultural historians have called our age of "post-modernity." As post-moderns, we have lost much of the innocence or bright-eyed optimism that was bequeathed to us by the Enlightenment. Still hopeful about the future, we are also suspicious of all grandiose or sure-fire visions of the future. Thanks to the progenitors of the "hermeneutics of suspicion" such as Nietzsche, Freud, Marx, we have come to realize the limits and the corruptions of reason and the human heart; in our noblest and most reasoned efforts to know the truth and fashion our world, in every effort to interpret the revelation given us by God, there is the worm of *ideology* – the ever lurking propensity to use our "truth" as a means of assuring our own advantage or control over that of others. Ideology stalks our noblest ideals and projects. As Walter Benjamin has said, "Every work of civilization [we could add, every work of religion] is at the same time a work of barbarism" (in Tracy 1987a, 69).

Such ideological abuse of religion is not just an "error" that can be pointed out and neatly removed. It is, rather, a "systemic distortion" (Tracy 1987a, 73). We cannot defend ourselves against such distortions by ourselves. We need others – the insights and perspectives of others who look at the world differently than we do, who can look at our visions of truth from a critical standpoint outside our circle, who perhaps can tell us how our "truth" has excluded or victimized them. We must, again, *learn* from others, so they can point out our distortions, our self-centered abuse of the truth that has been given us. Combining the insights of Max Müller and Walter Benjamin, we can say, "Those who know one, turn that one into a work of barbarism."

But our heightened awareness of the *need* to learn from others does not diminish our realization of the *difficulty* of doing so. As stated above, every interreligious encounter reveals how utterly different we really are and how much our understanding of the other is limited and clouded by our own perspectives; we are always looking into, rather than from out of, the other religion. If we somehow trust that we can look from within and genuinely understand, how might we act on this trust?

One way of answering that hermeneutical question lies along the lines of

David Tracy's *analogical imagination*. Tracy states succinctly what this means for interreligious dialogue:

> The phrase can remind conversation partners that difference and otherness once interpreted *as* other and *as* different are thereby acknowledged as in some way possible and, in the end, analogous . . . Authentic analogical language is a rare achievement since it attempts the nearly impossible: an articulation of real differences as genuinely different but also similar to what we already know (1987a, 93).

Tracy is inviting us to let our imaginations have free play as we attempt to "pass over" to the differences in the other religions; entering into these differences we may well discover that the very strangeness and difference becomes for us an unthought-of *possibility*. What was foreign, perhaps threatening, now becomes an invitation. The "other" in its otherness becomes a *disclosure* of new possibility, new truth. The other becomes analogical: both dissimilar and similar at the same time. In Tracy's words:

> In the to-and-fro movement of the game of conversation where the question or subject matter is allowed to "take over," we learn to abjure our constant temptation to control all reality by reducing all difference to the "same" (viz., what "we" already believe). In that same to-and-fro movement of conversation, we learn to allow the other, the different, to become other *for us* – i.e., as a genuinely *possible* mode-of-being-in-the-world, *as* other, *as* different, *as* possible, thus as a similarity-in-difference, an analogy (Tracy 1987b, 18).

Tracy's advice helps, but we feel the need for more concrete direction. How to put this analogical imagination into practice? Where do we start? – Answers to such practical questions can be found, I suggest, in the new context for interreligious dialogue that is presented by our contemporary world.

A new context and *kairos* for dialogue

The title of a recently published book by David Lochhead captures what mainline Christian churches are growing aware of: a "dialogical imperative" (Lochhead 1988). No doubt, this imperative is fed by the more philosophical considerations we have already mentioned: given the "lack of foundations," dialogue is the only show in town for an authentic pursuit of truth, and given the post-modern awareness of ideology, we have to talk with others to keep ourselves from turning "truth" into tools of oppression. There are also more expressly religious and theological reasons why the Second Vatican Council and recent statements of the World Council of Churches have pointed to interreligious dialogue as an imperative for all Christians (*Nostra Aetate, Guidelines*).

Two pivotal Christian beliefs convince Christians that dialogue is no longer a frill that can be pursued on Sunday afternoon when the rest of the chores are done, but something that pertains to the essence of Christian life. (*a*) The God of Abraham and of Jesus is a God whose love and revealing activity are universal and not to be confined to any one period or people; this means that there is most likely revelatory "gold in the hills" of other religions. (*b*) Also, if the entire law and the prophets are indeed summarized in the law of love of neighbor, then respecting and listening to our non-Christian neighbors has a clear priority over subjecting them to doctrinal claims about the finality of Christ and the inadequacy of extra-biblical religion. The ethics of love takes precedence over the doctrine of uniqueness.

Recognizing the validity of these reasons for the dialogical imperative, I want to suggest that our present-day world confronts us with an even greater and more urgent need for interreligious cooperation and conversation. It is a need that not only places dialogue in the center stage of every religion's concern but, in doing so, provides new opportunities for an even richer, more fruitful interreligious encounter. I am talking about the need for *liberation*.

Liberation: demanding and facilitating dialogue

Somewhat audaciously I am taking up the battered question of a "common core" within all religions. Today, most authorities have long dismissed this question as either impossible (we can never tell) or dangerous (the common core is defined by *me* for *you*). Certainly I do not want to resurrect the quest for a neatly defined "common essence" within all religions that can be found if we just scratch away the differing cultural accretions (Toynbee 1956). And yet, with others, I believe that although the religions of the world are apples and oranges and are more different than they are alike, still there is a quality of "fruit-fulness" that characterizes them all and out of which a "common ground" for shared conversation can be established.

What this commonality is, is hard to find or define. Some still look for it in the depths (or heights) of mystical experience (Merton 1968, 311, 315; Steindl-Rast, 1987). Others find it in the shared concern of all religions to move their followers from ego-centeredness to Reality-centeredness (Hick 1981, 464–7; Tracy 1987a, 84, 89–90). Vatican II's *Nostra aetate* holds to the more traditional and cautious assertion that all religions deal with common questions and concerns that have weighed on humankind since its birth. Revisionist theologians would seem to concur when they claim that there is a "common human experience" that serves as the sounding-board and criterion for the truth-claims of all religions (Ogden 1972; Tracy 1975, 43–63).

I suggest that our contemporary world enables us, not so happily, to lend precision to this quest for what might be common to our varied religious pursuits. Today there are particular, concrete questions, dangers, problems that, willy-nilly, are confronting all religions and demanding responses from them. They are questions that transcend cultural and religious differences, and if they do not require the religions to look at each other, they certainly require them all to look in the same direction. They touch *all* religions because they are the kind of questions that not only demand immediate attention but cannot be answered, so it seems, without some kind of transformation of the human species, without some kind of new vision or new way of understanding who we are as humans and how we are to live on this dizzying, threatened planet. In calling for a radically different way of viewing our world and acting in it, in confronting the limits of the human condition as we know it, they are *religious* questions – questions that every religion either has tried to answer, or will want to answer, or will be required to answer.

What is common to these cross-cultural, cross-religious questions is that all of them, in different ways, are calling for some form of this-worldly, earthly (as opposed to purely spiritual) *liberation*. Our contemporary world is a world aware, as never before so it seems, of oppression – oppression in an array of horrible forms. It is, in other words, a world painfully aware of the need for liberation, for breaking bonds, for preserving, restoring, fostering life. I am suggesting, therefore, that *liberation* – what it is and how to achieve it – constitutes a new arena for the encounter of religions. Briefly, I will list (more is not possible or necessary at the moment) the forms of oppression and needed liberation that can gather all religions into a new community of concern and conversation.

A world in need of liberation

1. *Liberation from physical suffering.* Certainly most of us are familiar with – to the point, perhaps, of immunity – the appalling statistics about the vast numbers of people who suffer chronically from some form or forms of physical suffering because they are deprived of the most fundamental human necessities. They – and most painfully, their children – suffer because they do not have enough to eat, or do not have a balanced diet, or do not have a reliable or clean water supply, or must live in disease-infested conditions, or do not have access to needed medical care or supplies. We are told that the majority of our earth's population live in some such conditions.

For more and more people, such realities scream to heaven and to religious sensitivities. Whatever their tradition, religious believers are coming to feel that their religion must confront such basic physical needs and sufferings and that whatever salvation or enlightenment or *moksha* may mean, such beliefs have to say something about this kind of suffering. Granted that we have to bear with the effects of karma, granted that we will never realize the fulness of the kingdom, granted that *dukkha* adheres to the human condition, granted that there will be another life here or elsewhere – still, Hindus, Christians, Jews, Muslims, Buddhists are recognizing that if any of these traditional beliefs become the reason or occasion for ignoring or condoning such human suffering, then such beliefs lose their credibility. Even the most traditionally "other-worldly" religions are showing concern and trying to formulate some kind of response to our world's growing awareness of human suffering. Tables bare of bread and water can become the tables around which the religions of the world gather to talk and act.

2. *Liberation from socio-economic oppression.* The world of widespread physical suffering impinges all the more on our religious sensitivities when we face up to the further reality that most of these sufferings are not natural – that they are caused by the way human beings treat other human beings or use others for their own self-serving purposes. Oppression and injustice are chains that crisscross our globe, nationally and multi-nationally, and have become almost an "unavoidable" part of socio-economic and political structures. Forged as they often are in the kilns of racism and sexism, these chains keep vast portions of our national or global population in bondage, denying them a voice in the decisions of power and in determining their own lives. There is a vast "underbelly" of history – people who, in their victimization, produce the labor, the raw materials, the armies that have sustained the course of history.

Yet this "silent majority" of oppressed is, today, no longer silent. Centuries of injustice are erupting in the consciousness of Third World peoples and flowing into the conscience of the First and Second Worlds. As the final conference of the Ecumenical Association of Third World Theologians (EATWOT) in New Delhi, 1981, announced:

> Over against this dramatic picture of poverty, oppression, and the threat of total destruction, a new consciousness has arisen among the downtrodden. This growing consciousness of the tragic reality of the Third World has caused the irruption of exploited classes, marginalized cultures, and humiliated races. They are burst from the underside of history into the world long dominated by the West. It is an irruption expressed in revolutionary struggles, political uprisings, and liberation movements. It is an irruption of religious and ethnic groups looking for affirmation of their authentic identity, of women demanding recognition and equality, of youth protesting dominant systems and values. It is an irruption of all those who struggle for full humanity and for their rightful place in history (Torres and Fabella 1983, 195).

As the EATWOT theologians stated, this eruption is a challenge not only for Christianity but for all religions – a challenge that does seem to be transforming the consciousness of members of all religions as they realize that unless they can speak a word of protest against socio-political oppression and announce a message of liberation, their religious words will grow more and more feeble. The hope that Hans Küng has drawn from his experience of interreligious dialogue is shared by many: "Numerous conversations in the Far and Near East have convinced me that in the future all the great religions will foster a vital awareness of the guarantee of human rights, the emancipation of women, the realization of social justice, and the immorality of war" (1987, 241). Thus the need for socio-economic justice is calling all religions to a forum in which they all need to and want to speak.

3. *Liberation from nuclear oppression/holocaust.* There is another form of oppression even more pervasive than that of socio-economic injustice; it grips First, Second, and Third Worlds equally. The realization that the entire population of the planet could be snuffed out by the pressing of a few buttons by a few political figures – whose political and psychological judgment and saneness we often have good cause to question – terrorizes us all. For the first time in its history, the human race is capable of something never before possible: humanocide. Humanity is able to commit communal suicide. "We thought to go to the moon, to divine the bottom of the ocean, to become God, but never did we think to wipe out humanity as such" (Rapp 1985, 16).

Liberation from nuclear oppression, some would say, is the hour's most pressing and most communal issue; it touches and terrorizes all of us. Gordon Kaufman is right: "... the possibility of nuclear holocaust is the premier issue which our generation must face ... [it is among] the central and defining features of our lives as human beings in the so-called civilized world in the late twentieth century" (1985, 14,12). If then, as Einstein said, after the dropping of the first atom bomb, everything is different, it is also different for the religions of the world. As evinced in world-wide religious peace movements such as the World Conference of Religions for Peace, religious believers are recognizing that they cannot continue with their religious "as usuals" but must draw on the riches of their traditions to address the oppressive menace of war and nuclear conflict. Peace, understood as the overcoming of this nuclear oppression, is becoming a *universal religious symbol* that challenges and calls together all religions.

4. *Liberation from ecological disaster.* Some would argue that there is an even more menacing oppression that threatens our and especially the lives of our children. Today, not only is the human species unjustly exploiting and killing off its own, not only is it maddeningly on the brink of humanocide, but it is also strangling the source of all life – mother earth and the eco-system. The industrial revolution, which has brought such advantages to our species, has also created an altar of consumerism and profiteering on which daily the life-blood of mother earth is poured. Thomas Berry, one of the most forceful of earth-prophets, does not exaggerate: "Our industrial economy is closing down the planet in the most basic modes of its functioning. The air, the water, the soil are already in a degraded condition. Forests are dying on every continent. The seas are endangered. Aquatic life forms in lakes and streams and in the seas are contaminated. The rain is acid" (Berry 1985a, 4). For Berry, such ecological oppression should precede every other issue on the international and interreligious agenda:

For the first time we are determining the destinies of the earth in a comprehensive and irreversible manner. The immediate danger is not *possible* nuclear war but *actual* industrial plundering (ibid., 3)

The issue of inter-human tensions is secondary to earth-human tensions. If humans will not become functional members of the earth community, how can humans establish functional relationships among themselves? (Berry 1985b, 3–4).

However we might rank the need for ecological liberation, it clearly is another issue that stares all religions in the face and demands answers and actions and new visions.

Concern for the well-being of the planet is the one concern that hopefully will bring the nations [and religions] of the world into an inter-nation [and interreligious] community (Berry 1985b, 3).

If the need for socio-economic, nuclear, ecological liberation is *the* "common human experience" painfully present to all religions, if in light of this experience representatives of the different religious traditions are looking into their individual soteriologies and realizing that they have a liberating message to announce to the world, then we can indeed claim that the religions today are standing on a common ground on which they can construct a more fruitful dialogue. And if we consider that this liberation cannot be realized piecemeal, in this or that culture or nation, but must be a worldwide, interconnected effort, then it becomes clear that a new dialogue among religions is not only possible, it is absolutely *necessary*. Worldwide liberation calls for a worldwide religious dialogue. The religions must talk to each other not only, as John Cobb has announced, to undergo "mutual transformation" but to foster world-transformation.

Which brings us to our third interrogative – if we face this newly felt imperative for dialogue, *how* can we best respond to it?

How to dialogue?

Much useful advice has been given on the "rules for dialogue" (Swidler 1987, 13–16). Perhaps one of the simplest and most useable sets of guidelines can be found in Bernard Lonergan's "transcendental precepts" for human knowing and deciding (Lonergan 1975, 3–25; cf. Gregson 1985):

1. *Be attentive*. We must be open and able genuinely to listen to what the dialogue partner is saying, no matter how foreign or strange or false it might seem. This requires our being able to step outside of our own world and our own interests and convictions – not to give them up, but to see beyond them. One of the best "techniques" for attempting this is described by John Dunne as "passing over;" using our feelings and imagination, we try to follow the symbols and stories and world-views of

another culture or religion in order to enter and walk in its world. We allow, as it were, the other tradition to study us as much as we it (Dunne 1972, ix, 53).

2. *Be intelligent*. We must make the sincere effort to understand what we have experienced and heard. This, of course, is even more difficult and will call for even more stretching. Here something like David Tracy's "analogical imagination," as described above, can serve us well.

3. *Be reasonable*. This is the step many of the rules for dialogue leave out or water down. We must try to evaluate the truth or falsity, the rightness or wrongness, of what we have understood. Without such effort to judge, dialogue becomes a purely academic pastime or innocuous chit-chat – aimed perhaps at understanding the world but providing no energy to change it. And yet, in the interreligious conversation, this transcendental principle is as dangerous as it is necessary; we noted above how easily and unconsciously we can impose our criteria of right or wrong on another. We need some kind of *shared* criteria or common ground, which, however, cannot be an ontological, unchangeable *foundation*, but must be created or discovered as shared "shaky ground" within the dialogue itself. Yet as we asked earlier, how go about this creation or discovery?

4. *Be responsible and change if you must*. What we have understood and judged to be true and good lays claim on us. If dialogue is to be honest and fruitful, we must respond to these claims. Having come to new insights, having identified the good where we did not expect it, we must live those insights and do that good. This may well mean changing certain previous beliefs, attitudes, practices. It may mean, in Cobb's terms, transformation, even the kind we didn't plan on (Cobb, 1982). Dialogue without this possibility of conversion is like a sleek aircraft that can take us anywhere but is not allowed to land.

Conditions for the possibility of fruitful interreligious dialogue

Clearly, the obstacles to living out these transcendental principles for dialogue are many. Overcoming the obstacles is a matter of experience, perseverance, and increasing skill. I would like to suggest two conditions which, if fulfilled, will facilitate the "art of dialogue" and will help remove the roadblocks. In fact, I am tempted to state that unless these conditions are met, dialogue is bound to bog down in entrenched or imposed positions.

First of all, religious believers cannot approach the table of dialogue with claims (on or below the table!) of having "the final word," or the "definitive revelation," or the "absolute truth," or the "absolute savior." Such claims stymie each of the transcendental principles: (*a*) How can we be genuinely *attentive* to what is different when our final norm has judged what is different to be inferior? (*b*) How can we freely and with abandon apply an analogical imagination to *understand* new possibilities when our final and unsurpassable revelation has excluded any worthwhile possibilities better than our own? (*c*)

In trying to make interreligious *evaluations* of truth and value, doesn't a definitive revelation meant to fulfill all others oblige us "in God's name" to impose our criteria on all others? (*d*) Finally, how can we *change* and endorse the differing visions of other religious figures if ours is the absolute savior, before whom every other religious knee must bend? – It would seem, therefore, that the revision of traditional understandings of "the uniqueness of Christ and Christianity" (together with similar understandings of the uniqueness of the Qur'an or of Krishna or of Buddha) is a condition for the possibility of fruitful dialogue.

Such a statement rankles many. Let me clarify what is intended. In questioning absolute or final truth claims, I am not at all questioning the necessity of entering the dialogue with firm convictions, with personal commitments to what one holds to be true and sacred, and with a universal message. Such clear, strong positions are the stuff of dialogue. But I *am* suggesting that in order for our commitment to be full and our claims to be clear and universal, they need not be final, superior, unsurpassable. For something to be *really* true, it need not be the *only* truth; conversely, to allow for *many* truths does not automatically permit *any*. What I am trying to say is more clearly lived than explained. Langdon Gilkey describes it as the paradox of practice that is required of any believer in our world of religious pluralism: we must be *absolutely* committed to positions that we know are *relative*. How to combine such absolute personal commitment with a recognition of the relativity of all religious forms and figures is one of the central challenges and responsibilities of religious believers today (Gilkey 1987, 44–50).

I venture to propose another condition for the possibility of authentic dialogue that is, on the other end of the spectrum, even more controversial than the first, for it carries the appearance of a veiled foundationalism. Picking up another pivotal element in Lonergan's analysis of the dynamics of cognitional structure, but moving in a direction different from Lonergan, I would suggest that for dialogue to really work it should, ideally, be "founded" (dangerous word!) on a conversion shared by all participants. Lonergan speaks about conversion as the foundation for applying his transcendental principles to theology: an *intellectual conversion*, by which we realize that knowing is not a matter of hearing or taking a look but of appropriating the process of experiencing, understanding and judging; a *moral conversion*, by which we attempt to *do* and live up to the truth we affirm; and especially, *religious conversion*, by which we "fall in love unrestrictedly" with the Mystery of the true and the good and so become empowered to know it and live it (Lonergan 1975, 101–24, 267–93). With his religious conversion, which sublates intellectual and moral conversion, Lonergan ends up with a form of mystical experience as the foundation of religious dialogue. This is where I want to shift directions.

Rather than calling for a common religious or mystical conversion as the starting point of dialogue, I would suggest, in light of our present *kairos* of "liberation" that presses on all religions, that religious believers begin their conversations with a common moral conversion by which they commit themselves to addressing and removing the sufferings of our race and of our planet. A shared commitment and a shared praxis toward promoting justice and socio-economic, nuclear, and ecological liberation would be the starting point (not the absolute foundation) that would enable religious believers to be attentive to, understand, and judge each other and so transform each other and the world. Let me explain how such a *liberation-centered* (or soteriocentric) model for dialogue might work.

A liberation-centered model for interreligious dialogue

I am well aware (or, I think I am) that what I am proposing as a *center* may sound like, or easily develop into, a *foundation*; and that opens the door to the danger of imperialism, for it is usually the people with the power who determine the foundation. So I want to stress that when I hold up conversion to the suffering and commitment to liberation as the starting point for dialogue, I am *proposing* not *imposing*. It is a proposal which I believe representatives from all religious traditions have accepted or will accept. The awareness of oppression and of the need for liberation is permeating and challenging religious consciousness throughout the world. The issues, as I argued above, are *religious*, for their solutions call for the energy and hope of religious values and visions; Hindus, Buddhists, Christians are realizing with increasing clarity that unless they respond to the "cries of the oppressed," they will be judged by the world as narcissistic pastimes or as opium.

Furthermore, as believers allow the plight of the poor and the call for liberation to illumine their scriptures and traditions, as they review their soteriologies in the light of our world's oppressions, they realize that they *do* have a liberative word to speak, a message for the suffering planet. I have tried to argue elsewhere that all religions can endorse a soteriocentric model for liberation because all of them, in different ways and degrees, contain a "soteriocentric core," a concern and vision for the welfare of humanity in this world. The models for human welfare and liberation admittedly differ, often drastically – and here we have the stuff of dialogue – but there is a shared concern that human beings be changed and saved, in this world (Knitter 1987b). Whether this is indeed the case, whether there is a soteriocentric core or concern within all religions that would enable a liberation-centered dialogue, can be known, of course, only within the dialogue itself.

Granting that significant numbers of representatives from various traditions can endorse a liberation-centered dialogue, how would it function? I suggest that it might profitably follow the turns of Juan Luis Segundo's hermeneutical circle, which he proposed as a liberation-centered model for revisioning Christian theology (Segundo 1975, 7–9).

According to Segundo, the preliminary "warm-up exercise" for the dialogue would call on all participants to train themselves in a wary attitude of *hermeneutical suspicion*. Before approaching each other, they would try to train

and tune themselves to detect where it is in their own beliefs and practices
and scriptural interpretations they have turned belief into ideology. They
need to prepare themselves for what dialogue will most likely reveal to them –
instances where they have used their religion or sold out their original vision
to "adjust" to the *status quo*, to curry the favor of the mighty, to hold the reins
of dominance over others. That ideology inevitably creeps into all religious
consciousness and practice is not the greatest of evils; far more dangerous is it
to be unaware or to deny that this is the plight of all religion, including one's
own. With a healthy dose of hermeneutical suspicion, then, we are warmed
up for dialogue.

But we are still not ready for the actual conversation with other religious
believers. What the liberation theologians say of Christian theology applies to
interreligious dialogue – *dialogue is always a second step* (Boff 1987, 23;
Gutiérrez, 1973, 11). Here is the hinge-pin of the soteriocentric model for
dialogue: we begin not with conversations about doctrine or ritual, nor even
with prayer or meditation (though all these elements are essential to the effort
to pass over to each other's traditions); rather, we begin with some form of
liberative praxis. We engage in efforts to liberate ourselves or others or our
planet from whatever form of oppression we agree to be pressing in our
immediate context – and we do so, not separately in our different religious
camps, but *together*.

This will require that as Hindus or Buddhists or Jews we work together in
trying to identify and understand the cause of the oppression or suffering we
are facing; we attempt some kind of shared socio-economic analysis of the
problem and what might be the solution; admittedly the solutions we discuss
will be inspired by our different religious convictions. Then we roll up our
sleeves together to act – to do whatever we think needs to be done. This will,
of course, require that we work with and especially *learn from* those who are
the oppressed and suffering. *Liberative praxis means identifying with and
learning from the struggling poor*; it recognizes what has been called the
"hermeneutical privilege" or the "epistemological priority" of the struggling
poor – that unless we are listening to the voice of their experience, our efforts
to understand our world and our religious traditions will be vitally maimed.

With the oppressed, then, and as members of different religious
communities, we work for justice or for peace or for ecological sustainability.
Such acting will gather our differing communities into a common community
of shared courage, frustration, anger, anguish; it will bring us together in the
common experience of fear, of danger, perhaps of imprisonment and even
martyrdom. It will also join us in shared success and victory in changing the
structures of oppression into communities of justice, cooperation, unity.

Such liberative praxis, with its peaks and its pits, will be the matrix of – and
imperative for – our dialogical *reflection*. Under the momentum of praxis, the
hermeneutical circle moves to reflection, discussion, study, prayer, meditation. But in a liberation-centered method of dialogue, such pursuits will not

be done only in our separated religious camps but together. Having acted together, Buddhists and Christians and Muslims now reflect and talk together about their religious convictions and motivations. Here is where the partners in dialogue can enter into their scriptures and doctrines and explain not only to themselves but to others what it is that animates and guides and sustains them in their liberative praxis.

What has been the experience of Christian theology of liberation might well be realized in interreligious dialogue – that when we reflect on our religious heritage on the basis of a praxis of commitment to the poor and oppressed, we find ourselves "bringing forth new treasures" from old treasures; we see and hear and understand our scriptures and our doctrines with new eyes and a new heart. In a soteriocentric dialogue, this can happen interreligiously – we can understand each others' scriptures and beliefs anew. Having heard and seen, for instance, how the Four Noble Truths or the nirvanic experience of *pratitya-samutpada* are enabling and directing Buddhist partners in the transformation of village life in Sri Lanka, Christians can come to appreciate and appropriate such beliefs/experiences in genuinely new and fruitful ways. And Buddhists will better grasp the Kingdom of God or resurrection-faith of Christians having experienced how it sustains their efforts for justice or their readiness to risk.

This is how we might provide concrete substance for Tracy's analogical imagination. Focusing our imaginations on how we can better cooperate in working for liberation and how we do so as different religious believers, we can better awaken to new *possibilities* in the amazingly different ways each of us is inspired and directed in our commitment to justice and life. As a Christian who shared Gandhi's commitment to socio-political transformation, I can "imagine" more readily the new possibilities for *my* religious practice in the Gita's challenge to "act without seeking the fruits of my actions."

The base Christian communities of Latin America can serve as a practical model for carrying out a soteriocentric interreligious dialogue. In these small grass-roots gatherings, Christians have met to re-read their scriptures and their beliefs in light of their oppression and their efforts to overcome it – and in the process what had been a church of the *status quo* is experiencing new life and vision. In the interreligious encounter, what we can envision and what is already taking place in Asia are *base human communities* – communities which gather people not of one religious tradition but people of different religious beliefs who share *one commitment* to overcoming injustice and working with the oppressed. In these communities, the same dynamic as that of the base Christian communities can and is taking place – scriptures are coming alive, doctrine makes sense, religious experience is deepened – between Buddhists and Christians and Hindus. Here is hope for a new form of interreligious dialogue, based on a *common conversion* to the poor and suffering.

And if the blood of martyrs is the seed of hope, we can expect ever greater life from these base human communities, for in Sri Lanka they have had their first martyr. In November 1987 Fr Michael Rodrigo OMI, one of the most committed and successful promoters of base human communities of Christians and Buddhists, was murdered after celebrating mass with Sri Lankan villagers. His liberation-centered efforts and successes in promoting dialogue and peace between Buddhists, Hindus, and Christians stood in the way of those who preferred military solutions to Sri Lanka's divisions. His commitment to dialogue and justice remains an inspiration and a "dangerous memory" (Rodrigo 1987).

A liberation-centered solution for Christian exclusivism

If a liberation-centered approach to dialogue supplies one of the conditions for the fruitfulness of dialogue – by providing a common conversion or concern on which to construct the common ground of understanding and cooperation – can it also help us fulfil the other condition for fruitful dialogue: the removal of exclusive claims to absolute or final truth? I think it can. In the final part of this chapter I will address my fellow Christians and try to show how a soteriocentric approach to other religions can aid Christians in finding that difficult middle ground between a traditional Christian exclusivism or inclusivism on the one hand and a sloppy, debilitating liberal relativism on the other.

Especially over the past decade, Christian theologians have realized the inadequacies of even "liberal" attitudes toward other faiths which, having abandoned the exclusivist claims of Christianity as the only true religion, still hold to Christianity as the inclusive fulfillment of all other religions (Hick/ Knitter, 1987). Yet to move beyond these traditional views, based as they are on confessional views of Christ, would seem to break continuity with Christian tradition and cut the theologian off from his/her roots in the *sensus fidelium*. Dare we cross what has been called a "theological Rubicon" to a pluralist attitude that recognizes the possible parity and validity of other religions alongside Christianity? A liberation-centered form of dialogue can help us make the crossing without losing our Christian maps.

Transcending Christian exclusivism/inclusivism

Especially from a Roman Catholic perspective, Christian theology of religions over the past decades has undergone an evolution that seems to point in the direction of what I am calling a liberation-centered model. In the 1960s and early 1970s (in Vatican II and in the WCC), there was a move *from ecclesiocentrism to christocentrism* in the churches' approach to other faiths. Theologians no longer talked about the church as the "necessary means of salvation" or of the need to make all peoples members (manifest or latent) of the church. The universal, cosmic Christ was the principle of salvation

(Knitter 1985, 121–30). In the 1970s and early 1980s some theologians began to move *from christocentrism to theocentrism.* They no longer insisted on Jesus Christ as the one mediator – or "constitutive cause" – of all salvation, which meant they no longer had to posit a hidden activity of the cosmic Christ within all other religions or surreptitiously to identify authentic believers in other traditions as "anonymous Christians." God, not necessarily Jesus Christ, was the center of the salvific universe (Knitter 1985, 145–204; Hick 1973). More recently, many of these same theologians (I'm certainly one of them) have grown aware of the "anonymous imperialism" or "theocentric foundationalism" in Christian approaches to other faiths based on the recognition of the one God of Jesus Christ working differently within all other religions.

Here is where a *soteriocentric* or salvation-centered model can carry forward the evolution in Christian attitudes. In this model, the center or the "Absolute," if we can still so speak, is not the church or Christ or even God but salvation or human liberation – the welfare of humanity and of this earth, the promotion of life and the removal of that which promotes death. In this model the guiding light or heuristic for understanding and evaluating other religious traditions is not the way they are able to be incorporated into the Christian ecclesial community, nor the way they show the hidden presence of and preparation for Christ, nor the way they "re-present" the same God revealed by Jesus the Nazarean – but rather, the way we find ourselves able to work with them to promote human welfare, the liberation of humanity and earth. In more expressly Christian terms, the framework for a Christian theology of religions is not church, Christ, or God but *soteria* or the kingdom of God. Of course church, Christ, God are not simply discarded or kept on the sidelines of dialogue; rather, they are "aufgehoben:" transformed and understood anew in their relation to the kingdom.

All this, I'm sure, triggers suspicions in the minds of many. Just how does "liberation" or "the kingdom of God" function as this new starting point for dialogue? Aren't we always using our own particular Christian understanding of human welfare? Does a soteriocentric dialogue become another, more subtle and therefore more pernicious, form of imposing our Christian "absolutes" or "foundations" on other faiths?

Certainly, as Christians, we hold to an understanding of human welfare given us by the Nazarean, grounded in his experience of God as Abba, transmitted in the church. As I said, in becoming soteriocentric we do not discard or compromise our allegiance to church, Christ, and God. In a sense, we remain ecclesio- and christo- and theocentric, for in Jesus, in his experience of God, and in his community we have found a vision and a power of liberation that has transformed our lives and promises to transform this world. We are, in other words, "absolutely" committed to this Christian vision: we devote our total energies to it; yes, we hope, we are willing to give our lives for it.

Despite this "absolute" commitment, however, we know that even the vision given us in Christ is "relative." And we know this not simply from our own experience that the kingdom is always more than we can ever realize but also from the way Jesus himself relativized everything he or his church would say in the essentially *eschatological* character of his message. Though always "already," the kingdom was also always "not yet." Because of the "already" we are fully committed to this kingdom and we passionately represent it in the dialogue; but because of the "not yet" we are also humbly, readily open to other manifestations of that kingdom – to other understandings of what makes for human welfare. *Soteria* or the kingdom of God, therefore, serves us as a criterion for understanding and judging other traditions, but never in a final or absolute way. It requires us always to be open to and stand criticized by their understanding and judgments of us.

There is another reason why "human welfare" or the kingdom of God can serve participants in religious dialogue as a workable but non-absolutist criterion for conversation. Not only is *soteria*, like "God," a mystery in the sense that it is always more than what we can know or realize; also, the manner in which it is able to be partially known and realized precludes any one tradition from having a privileged position in stating what it means or will be. What I am getting at has to do with the "hermeneutical privilege of the poor." In the actual process of dialogue, what decides whether a particular symbol or belief or practice does promote liberation and welfare is not simply how strongly a religion has claimed that it does, but what the poor and oppressed think of it – how much they find that it frees them or promotes their welfare. Any claims of truth must come out of this listening to the oppressed. Thus, the voice of the oppressed becomes a safeguard against absolutizing or finalizing any religious claim.

Knowing and working toward liberation or the kingdom of God, then, is a continuous process; there are no final or absolute expressions of it. The way this process works – and the way we grow in knowledge of *soteria* and of what does or does not promote liberation – is through a twofold conversation: between our different religious communities and between our communities and those in need of liberation. Every religion must dialogue with other religions and with the oppressed.

A soteriocentric Christology

As is implied in the above, a non-absolutist Christian approach to other religions will require a non-absolutist Christology. Our liberation-centered or soteriocentric perspective can help us, I suggest, work toward such a christological revision. A soteriocentric Christology, which stresses what Jesus preached and how he acted over who or what he was, can throw needed light on three areas: the content of Jesus' original message, how to understand all the wonderful things his followers said of him, and what it means to follow him today.

Christology should be soteriocentric because so was Jesus. As Jon Sobrino reminds us, what constituted "the absolute" for Jesus – his central concern and that in the light of which he judged the meaning and value of everything else – was neither a particular notion he had of himself or of his role nor a particular doctrine of God; it was, rather, *the Kingdom of God* (Sobrino 1987, 75–6). As is clear in all the Synoptics, the core content, "the master-symbol," of Jesus' preaching was the *basileia tou theou* (Mackey 1979, 124–42). And whatever else the kingdom of God might contain in this life and in the next, it undeniably called for a different way of living and ordering society in this world. According to contemporary New Testament interpretation, this was Jesus' primary intent: to bring about a kingdom of life, a society based on love, unity, justice – especially for those of his society who were most deprived of life and love and justice: the poor, the sick, the sinners (Echegary 1984; Nolan 1978; Cassidy 1978). "Jesus' listeners understood one thing perfectly: while the force behind the kingdom was the force of God, the reality of the kingdom was something to be achieved on earth, so that society as a whole would reflect the will of God: 'Thy kingdom come. Thy will be done *on earth* as it is in heaven'" (Segundo 1985, 88). This was Jesus' "absolute" – that God's kingdom be realized on earth as it is in heaven. Everything else took a second place.

Whatever Jesus' self-understanding was, it took shape in relation – and in subordination – to this kingdom of love and justice. Scholars tell us that we perhaps come closest to Jesus' own sense of identity and mission when we view him as a prophet – as a servant of the kingdom. Yet he also seems to have understood himself as the *eschatological* or final prophet (Schillebeeckx 1979, 154–229, 441–515). This underlines what is otherwise evident in the Gospels – that Jesus felt his message and role was essential to bringing about this kingdom, that people had to "take sides" on what he was announcing. Still, this does not mean that he was setting himself above the kingdom or that he was limiting possibilities of knowing and working for the kingdom to himself. As Sobrino and Segundo insist, we are doing Jesus a disservice, to say the least, when we so absolutize him as to distract from our own responsibilities to work for and to recognize the kingdom of God wherever it might be (Sobrino 1984, 43; Segundo 1985, 186f.).

After the resurrection, when the proclaimer rightfully and necessarily became the proclaimed, Christianity became exposed to the danger of a "Jesusology" or a "christological reduction" that reduces God and the kingdom of God to Jesus and the church (Sobrino 1987, 20; 1984, 41). If Jesus is so absolutized, Christian existence is understood primarily as a confession of or a relationship with Jesus rather than as a commitment to working for the kingdom. We forget that Jesus "does not himself exhaust the totality of meditation of the will of God" and does not "represent the accomplishment of God's final will" (Sobrino 1984, 41–2; cf. 1987, 51). In our full commitment to him, we must be open to other expressions, other possibilities of realizing human welfare and liberation.

In interpreting all the things that were said about Jesus after the resurrection, a soteriocentric Christology, therefore, will give a certain "hermeneutical privilege" to the image of Jesus-as-prophet; or, his role as prophet will serve as a healthy "hermeneutics of suspicion" as we try to understand and apply the meaning of all the christological titles. This seems only fitting – that what seems to have been Jesus' own sense of mission and "the earliest Jesus kerygma" (Ogden 1982, 115–18; Schillebeeckx, 154–229; Dunn 1980, 253–4) should guide us in our interpretations of subsequent statements about him. Holding to Jesus primarily as prophet and servant of the kingdom, we will make clear that the ultimate intent of the litany of titles that were lavished on him was not to extol him in and for himself; it was not to make him a cult figure – the new top God to take over from the Greco-Roman pantheon. Rather, Jesus was glorified in order that his mission might be carried on – in order that the kingdom might be realized. In the early communities' spontaneous proclamation of Jesus as "Lord," "Savior," "Word," "Son of God," the *primary* intent, I suggest, was not to glorify him or give him primacy but to carry on his work. If he was afforded primacy, it was because his early followers felt this to be a necessary part of continuing his kingdom-project.

As Seiichi Yagi has perceptibly argued, when we look at the existential reality of the pre-ecclesial *basileia tou theou* and at the *risen Christ* of the early community of Jesus-followers, we realize we are talking about the same reality (Yagi 1987, 129–30). Guided by the hermeneutical priority of Jesus-as-prophet, therefore, we are reminded that if all the christological developments after the resurrection brought about a necessary and happy christocentrism in the community's life and worship, this christocentrism must never overshadow or stand in the way of Jesus' own "kingdom-centrism." Devoted to Jesus the prophet and given to working for the justice of the kingdom, we will be suspicious of any such overshadowings, for we well know that when it becomes more important to "bend all knees" before the sovereignty of Jesus than to work for the justice of his kingdom, Christianity all too easily slips not only into an other-worldly pietism but into a this-worldly imperialism.

A soteriocentric Christology, with its hermeneutical focus on Jesus as prophet, will also help us grasp what it really means to be faithful to the New Testament's and to tradition's christological confessions. Titles such as "the only-begotten Son of God" and "one Mediator" were not meant to supply the community with definitions of Jesus' ontological status by which they could then rule out all other contenders; the language of such titles was not primarily dogmatic or philosophical. It was, rather, performative – *action language* – meant to call the disciples of Jesus and all peoples to commit themselves to the work of love and justice, to live as Jesus lived, to devote themselves to realizing the kingdom. The purpose of "professing" is to follow, not the other way around. Fidelity to the New Testament confessions about Jesus, therefore, essentially means acting with and like Jesus, not insisting that he is above all others. In fact, the only way we can really know what our christological professions and titles really mean is by following Jesus and working for justice and love. As the liberation theologians tell us, orthopraxis should take first place to orthodoxy – though the two aspects of religious life cannot be separated: orthodoxy is meant to serve and foster orthopraxis; orthopraxis calls for orthodoxy.

The implications of a soteriocentric Christology for a new approach to interreligious dialogue are evident. If fidelity to our traditional confessions is primarily a matter of following Jesus the prophet-servant of the kingdom, we will be, at least theoretically, open to the possibility of other prophets. What matters most is that the kingdom be promoted, not that Jesus maintain the primacy. Therefore if in the dialogue we encounter other prophets who are promoting human welfare and salvation – even in ways utterly unexpected and different from what we have seen in Jesus – we will rejoice and learn and cooperate. But does this allow Jesus to remain the *final* prophet? Again, the emphasis is on *prophet*, not final. Proclaiming him *as final* means that we are totally committed to his vision; following him *as prophet* means that we remain totally open to wherever and through whomever the kingdom is forming and salvation is realized.

To see more exactly how it works, we can apply this soteriocentric, "prophet-first" interpretation to one of the apparently most exclusivistic texts of the New Testament: "There is no salvation in anyone else, for there is no other name in the whole world given to humanity by which we are to be saved" (Acts 4:12). The context itself already warns us against using this passage to rule all other witnesses out of court before we can present Jesus. The question at issue was "not one of comparative religions but of faith-healing" – that is, in whose power had Peter and John just healed the crippled man (Robinson 1979, 105), and more broadly, in whose power had the disciples undergone the transformation that was so evident to their fellow Jews? The passage delivers a clear answer: not Peter and John's own power, but the power contained in the name and reality of Jesus the Christ.

The intent of the language then is not philosophical/theological – to define Jesus in relation to other religious leaders; rather, it is clearly praxic, performative – to call others to recognize and accept the power that is available to them in this Jesus (Stendahl 1981; Starkey 1982, 69–71). Other passages from the story make this intent evident: "In the power of that name this man stands before you perfectly sound" (Acts 4:10) . . . "It is his name and trust in this name that has strengthened the limbs of this man" (Acts 3:16). The implication is evident: if we can trust in the power of this name, our limbs can also be strengthened for tasks that presently seem impossible, as impossible as that a crippled person should walk. Acts 3:23 makes it even clearer that Peter was talking about the power of Jesus the prophet: "Anyone who does not listen to that prophet [foretold by Moses] shall be ruthlessly cut off from the people."

Again, such language is telling us that we run great risk if we do not listen to and follow this prophet. "No other name," as performative, action language, is really a positive statement in its negative couching: it tells us that all peoples must listen to this Jesus; it does *not* tell us that no one else should be listened to or learned from. The stress, then, is on the *saving power* mediated by the name of Jesus, not on the exclusivity of the name. If in our dialogue we find that this power of liberation is experienced through other names, then the spirit of this passage would call us to be open to them. Whatever can genuinely heal a cripple mediates this power. Certainly for Jesus – as well as for his early followers – the most important thing was that cripples be healed, not that they be healed only through the name of Jesus.

If in our interreligious dialogue we can agree that our first concern is not the primacy of our names or the accuracy of our doctrines but, rather, the healing of cripples, we will grow in the ability to understand and to call on each others' names. And in this process, our race and our earth will be healed.

References

Berger, Peter, 1981, "The Pluralistic Situation and the Coming Dialogue between the World Religions," *Buddhist-Christian Studies*, 1:31–41

Berry, Thomas, 1985a, "Economics as a Religious Issue," in *Riverdale Papers X*, Riverdale, NY: Riverdale Center for Religious Research

—, 1985b, "The Cosmology of Peace," in *Riverdale Papers X*, Riverdale, NY: Riverdale Center for Religious Research

Bernstein, Richard, 1983, *Beyond Objectivism and Relativism: Science, Hermeneutics, and Praxis*, Philadelphia: University of Pennsylvania Press

Boff, Leonardo and Clodovis, 1987, *Introducing Liberation Theology*, Maryknoll: Orbis Books and London: Burns and Oates

Cassidy, Richard J., 1978, *Jesus, Politics, and Society: A Study of Luke's Gospel*, Maryknoll: Orbis Books

Cobb, John, Jr, 1982, *Beyond Dialogue: Toward a Mutual Transformation of Christianity and Buddhism*, Philadelphia: Fortress Press

Dunn, James D. G., 1980, *Christology in the Making*, London: SCM Press and Philadelphia: Westminster Press

Dunne, John, 1972, *The Way of All the Earth*, Notre Dame University Press and London: SPCK

Echegary, Hugo, 1984, *The Practice of Jesus*, Maryknoll: Orbis Books

Fiorenza, Francis Schüssler, 1984, *Foundational Theology: Jesus and the Church*, NY: Crossroad

Gilkey, Langdon, 1987, "Plurality and Its Theological Implications," in *The Myth of Christian Uniqueness: Toward a Pluralistic Theology of Religions*, John Hick and Paul F. Knitter, eds., Maryknoll: Orbis Books and London: SCM Press, pp. 37–50

Gregson, Vernon, 1985, *Lonergan, Spirituality, and the Meaning of Religion*, Lanham, MD: University Press of America

Guidelines for Dialogue with People of Living Faiths and Ideologies, 1979, Geneva: WCC

Gutiérrez, Gustavo, 1973, *A Theology of Liberation*, Maryknoll: Orbis Books and London: SCM Press

Hick, John, 1973, *God and the Universe of Faiths*, NY: St. Martin's Press

—, 1981, "On Grading Religions," *Religious Studies*, 17:451–67

—, and Paul F. Knitter, eds, 1987, *The Myth of Christian Uniqueness: Toward a Pluralistic Theology of Religions*, Maryknoll: Orbis Books and London: SCM Press

Katz, Steven T., 1978, "Language, Epistemology, and Mysticism," in *Mysticism and Philosophical Analysis*, Steven T. Katz, ed., NY: Oxford University Press, pp. 22–74

—, ed., 1982, *Mysticism and Religious Traditions*, NY: Oxford University Press

Kaufman, Gordon D., 1985, *Theology for a Nuclear Age*, Philadelphia: Westminster

Knitter, Paul, 1985, *No Other Name? A Critical Survey of Christian Attitudes toward World Religions*, Maryknoll: Orbis Books and London: SCM Press

—, 1981, "Dialogue and Liberation: Foundations for a Pluralist Theology of Religions, *The Drew Gateway*, 58: 1–53.

Küng, Hans, 1987, "What is True Religion? Toward an Ecumenical Criteriology," in *Toward a Universal Theology of Religion*, Leonard Swidler, ed., Maryknoll: Orbis Books, pp. 231–50

Lindbeck, George, 1984, *The Nature of Doctrine: Religion and Theology in a Postliberal Age*, Philadelphia: Westminster Press

Lochhead, David, 1988, *The Dialogical Imperative*, Maryknoll: Orbis Books and London: SCM Press

Lonergan, Bernard, 1972, *Method in Theology*, NY: Herder & Herder and London: Darton Longman and Todd

Mackey, James P., 1979, *Jesus: The Man and the Myth*, London: SCM Press and NY: Paulist Press

Merton, Thomas, 1968, *The Asian Journal of Thomas Merton*, (Naomi Burton, et. al., eds), NY: New Directions Books and London: Sheldon Press

Nolan, Albert, 1978, *Jesus before Christianity*, Maryknoll: Orbis Books

Ogden, Schubert, 1972, "What is Theology?" *The Journal of Religion*, 52:22–40

—, 1982, *The Point of Christology*, NY: Harper & Row and London: SCM Press

Panikkar, Raimundo, 1978, *The Intrareligious Dialogue*, NY: Paulist Press

—, 1987a, "The Invisible Harmony: A Universal Theory of Religion or a Cosmic Confidence in Reality?" in *Toward a Universal Theology of Religion*, Leonard Swidler, ed., Maryknoll: Orbis, pp. 118–53

—, 1987b, "The Jordan, the Tiber, and the Ganges: Three Kairological Moments in Christic Self-Consciousness," in *The Myth of Christian Uniqueness: Toward a Pluralistic Theology of Religions*, John Hick and Paul F. Knitter, eds., Maryknoll: Orbis Books and London: SCM Press, pp. 89–116

Rapp, R., 1985, "Cultural Disarmament," *Interculture*, 89:14–33

Robinson, John A. T., 1979, *Truth is Two-Eyed*, London: SCM Press

Rodrigo, Michael, 1987, "Buddhism and Christianity: Toward a Human Future – An Example of Village Dialogue of Life," Paper presented at the Buddhist-Christian Conference, Berkeley, CA, August

Rorty, Richard, 1979, *Philosophy and the Mirror of Nature*, Princeton University Press

Schillebeeckx, Edward, 1979, *Jesus: An Experiment in Christology*, NY: Seabury Press and London: Collins

Segundo, Juan Luis, 1975, *Liberation of Theology*, Maryknoll: Orbis Books

—, 1985, *The Historical Jesus of the Synoptics*, Maryknoll: Orbis Books

Smith, Wilfred Cantwell, 1981, *Toward a World Theology*, Philadelphia: Westminster Press and London: Macmillan

Sobrino, Jon, 1984, *The True Church and the Poor*, Maryknoll: Orbis Books and London: SCM Press

—, 1987, *Jesus in Latin America*, Maryknoll: Orbis Books

Starkey, Peggy, 1982, "Biblical Faith and the Challenge of Religious Pluralism," *International Review of Missions*, 71:68–74

Stendahl, Krister, 1981, "Notes on Three Bible Studies," in *Christ's Lordship and Religious Pluralism*, Gerald H. Anderson and Thomas F. Stransky, eds, Maryknoll: Orbis Books, pp. 7–18

Steindl-Rast, David, 1987, "Who is Jesus Christ for Us Today?," in *The Christ and the Bodhisattva*, Donald S. Lopez, Jr, and Steven C. Rockefeller, eds, Albany: State University of New York Press, pp. 99–116

Swidler, Leonard, ed., 1987, *Toward a Universal Theology of Religion*, Maryknoll: Orbis Books

Toynbee, Arnold, 1956, "The Task of Disengaging the Essence from the Non-essentials in Mankind's Religious Heritage," in *An Historian's Approach to Religion*, London and NY: Oxford University Press, pp. 261–83

Torres, Sergio, and Virginia Fabella, eds, 1983, *The Irruption of the Third World: A Challenge to Theology*, Maryknoll: Orbis Books

Tracy, David, 1975, *Blessed Rage for Order: The New Pluralism in Theology*, NY: Seabury

—, 1987a, *Plurality and Ambiguity: Hermeneutics, Religion, Hope*, NY: Harper & Row and London: SCM Press

—, 1987b, "Christianity in the Wider Context: Demands and Transformations," *Religion and Intellectual Life*, 4:7–20

Yagi, Seiichi, 1987, "'I' in the Words of Jesus," in *The Myth of Christian Uniqueness: Toward a Pluralistic Theology of Religions*, John Hick and Paul F. Knitter, eds, Maryknoll: Orbis Books and London: SCM Press, pp. 117–34

The Thrust and Tenor of Our Conversations

—

Monika K. Hellwig

When the newly elected Pope Paul VI sat down, contrary to custom, to write his own inaugural encyclical (*Ecclesiam suam*, "His Church," 1963), his topic was the church, and his definition of the church was a meditative description of multidirectional dialogue. The Second Vatican Council, initiated by his predecessor, Pope John XXIII, and continued under Pope Paul VI, was based upon the same understanding, though implicitly. John XXIII in person engaged in dialogue both within the Catholic communion and outside it. In his encyclical letters he addressed invitations to serious conversation to the other Christians (*Ad cathedram Petri*, "Peter's Chair," 1959); to rich nations, industrialists and economists concerning world poverty (*Mater et magistra*, "Mother and Teacher," 1961); and the leaders of nations including those of the Communist bloc concerning peace and disarmament (*Pacem in terris*, "Peace on Earth," 1963). He met with the Patriarch of Constantinople, with the Archbishop of Canterbury, and with Nikita Krushchev's son-in-law, in each case reversing a previous policy of stony silence. He made special overtures to Jews and to the Patriarch of Moscow. He spoke with peasants in Portugal, prisoners at Regina Coeli prison, and the sick in Roman hospitals. It was a new style, and it drew enthusiastic response from all quarters.

The Second Vatican Council also met in a new style. Already Catholic observers had been sent to the World Council of Churches. Now observers from other churches were invited to participate at Vatican II. Many ecumenical and worldly subjects were explored: the old issues that divided the churches (in *Dei verbum*, "On Divine Revelation," 1965; in *Unitatis redintegratio*, "On Ecumenism," 1964; in *Orientalium ecclesiarum*, "On Eastern Catholic Churches," 1964; and in *Dignitatis humanae*, "On Religious Freedom," 1965); the new issues arising from modern technology and culture (in *Gaudium et spes*, "On the Church in the Modern World," 1965; in *Inter mirifica*, "On the Instruments of Social Communication," 1963; and in *Gravissimum educationis*, "On Christian Education," 1965); and the delicate questions concerning relations with those of other religions (in *Nostra aetate*, "On the Relationship of the Church to Non-Christian Religions," 1965; and *Ad gentes*, "On the Church's Missionary Activity," 1965).

All of this is startling to anyone familiar with the nineteenth- and early twentieth-century history of the Catholic Church – with the *Syllabus of Errors* of 1864, the First Vatican Council of 1869–70, and the Oath against Modernism applied from 1910 to the eve of Vatican II. Yet even more astonishing and consequential than the statements produced was the rediscovery of collegiality among the bishops, and therefore among the local churches, and the spreading of the sense of collegiality to the grassroots, giving rise to new bursts of local initiative. In Latin America, for instance, the Bishops' Conference at Medellin in 1968 gave official sanction to the grassroots initiatives of the basic Christian communities and to the far-reaching questions of liberation theology arising out of the experience and commitment of those communities.

Yet all of these developers leave a basic question hanging in the air – a question becoming more urgent now with the more autocratic style of Pope John-Paul II, the renewed dogmatism of the Congregation for the Doctrine of the Faith, and the retrenchment from ecumenical relations, lay involvement, women's participation, and local initiative. The question that hangs in the air is: what is dialogue and how is it related to the quest for truth? Clearly, there has been a widespread sense of disappointment over recent events in the institutional Catholic Church, even a certain sense of betrayal in the experience that the promises of Vatican II and its new style are not being fulfilled.

Not every speech or utterance makes a genuine conversation, and not every conversation constitutes dialogue such as the churches are seeking increasingly today. Speech or utterance may be in fact or also in intent a soliloquy. Much of the disappointment in and with the Catholic Church, even since Vatican II, has been along those lines; too often one has the sense of being in the presence of a sonorous monologue. Moreover, a conversation may be in the form of an exchange of ideas, information or viewpoints, and yet be in substance a one-way communication in exchange for total attention or receptivity moving in the other direction. In many parts of the world today education and political process have awoken people from an age-old social lethargy to a state of alert expectation. They have learned to be subjects of their own history, not the object of someone else's history. They have learned that mature humanity means participation in observation, evaluation and decision-making in all that shapes the society in which they live. There is little tolerance for any conversation that presents itself as an exchange but is in fact a one-way communication. Here again seems to be a source of resentment in and about the Catholic Church as it functions institutionally in our times.

There can also, of course, be conversations in which both sides, or all sides, speak but one or more understand the exchange merely as an argument. There may be the understanding that the truth is known already and the truth is clear and exclusive; therefore the point of the conversation is to persuade the other or others of their error. In this case a protagonist may listen extremely attentively, but only so as to show the error in the position presented. This kind of conversation the churches have long carried out under the rubric of apologetics. The pattern can be traced back to the second-century Apologists defending Christian faith against pagans and Jews. It is found with renewed passion after the sixteenth-century Reformation, where the protagonists defended their own Christian denomination against others, and it came into a whole new sphere with the Enlightenment and the demand to defend Christian particularity against the demands of universal reason – a task that preoccupies many thinkers still. But apologetics, like dogmatism in intra-church discussion, is not dialogue.

The true dialogue, for which many post-Enlightenment Christians feel an urgent need, is a continuing quest for truth and for a deeper, more comprehensive understanding on all sides. For many people in our times this seems to be a very lonely quest in which individuals engaging in dialogue with people of all persuasions find themselves inadvertently drifting further and further away from their community of origin. But even where it is a group project officially authorized by the institutional churches, those who participate often find that progress in the dialogue isolates them from the church that authorized the dialogue. This seems to be a common experience of those officially involved in Christian-Jewish dialogue, and not unusual for those involved in the bilateral consultations between churches.

The reason for this kind of tension seems to be that the dialogue itself brings a growth in understanding that is not shared by those who authorized it because they do not actually participate in the experience. In true dialogue there is both active and passive sharing of experience, viewpoint, understanding, hopes and concerns. It involves sharing particular histories and, through that, sharing a deeper appreciation and understanding of the symbols and rituals of one another's traditions. It involves, therefore, not only an exercise in understanding but also an extension of one's experience in empathy – in entering into the experience of others.

The goals of dialogue between persons of different faith-traditions seem basically to be three: to gain a friendly understanding of others, to enrich and round out one's appreciation of one's own faith tradition, and to establish a more solid foundation for community of life and action among persons of various traditions. The first of these seems to be the more obvious goal with which in most cases dialogue is explicitly begun. It may rest upon pleasant curiosity, or scholarly intent, or practical necessity to overcome obstacles to daily coexistence in the world. In any case, it is readily apparent that we ought to know others as they truly are and not in caricature, and to know them as they really are it is certainly necessary to enter into serious dialogue with them. It is always wise to assume that there is more to learn about others and that the most important truths about others are those which we can learn only when those others choose to reveal themselves, not those which we can learn by observing the others as objects.

While this urge to know more about others certainly justifies and explains itself in this way on its own grounds, those who have at any time engaged in more intensive dialogue with persons of other faith-traditions tend to seek further contacts of this kind with the additional goal of getting a new perspective and insight in their own tradition. It is inevitable that this will happen, because all our religious language is analogous. We cannot know or name the transcendent except by metaphors drawn from our human experience in its particular historical and cultural setting. But most believers become aware of this very slowly, if at all. Again and again we tend to a kind of idolatry that takes the image for the reality and the name for the essence. Dialogue with those outside the tradition is bound to challenge this in two ways: in explaining to the outsider one must reflect more critically on one's own beliefs, attitudes and practices, and must attempt a number of different ways to give intelligibility; in listening to the outsider with empathy and interest one discovers analogies and complementarities in the quest for the ultimate, and therefore also experiences a relativizing of the expression of that quest in one's own tradition.

A third goal, which is sometimes explicit, is that of establishing a more solid foundation for community of life and action among persons of various traditions. It cannot be the immediate goal but can only grow out of the other two. A common ground for action, for instance in matters of social justice or peace or routine administration of affairs in the larger society, can really be established only when there has been a growing appreciation for the values and worldview of the other tradition and a consequent renewal and relativizing of one's perception of one's own tradition. It is tempting but counter-productive to move swiftly to the third goal, establishing only a very superficial and flimsy common basis for action.

In order to have a solid basis of commonality, it seems to be important first to share one's ideals, one's vision, and to try to see and experience the ideals and vision of the others. It would seem that one of the common failures of human community and solidarity derives from the tendency to judge one's own group by the ideals of that group but to judge outsiders by their actual performance. The obvious result of such an evaluation is always a certain contempt, or at least supercilious condescension, towards the others. To be explicit and reflective in sharing one's own ideals with outsiders is necessarily a step to realizing how little those ideals are in fact implemented by one's own people. To be courteously attentive in trying to see the ideals and values of the others with their eyes is a necessary step towards an evaluation of the others that is truer to the reality of their lives. A sharing of ideals and values is the best way of finding what is really in common between two traditions.

There are, of course, many ways of sharing ideals and visions with others. There is first of all the reliving of one's history, one's story as a people. But there is also the sharing of the stories or histories of individuals within the tradition. Thus Catholicism makes a habit of telling the stories of the saints of the tradition in ways that outsiders as well as insiders of the tradition often find moving. Some Protestant groups set great store by personal witness in the form of telling one's own life or conversion story. Besides these historical accounts, there is also a sharing of vision and ideals by the telling of myths. Thus Greeks and Egyptians in ancient times, Hindus and Akan peoples in our own times, tell representative stories about the gods. And in most of our traditions there is a heritage of mixing the two – the historical and the mythical stories – using representative or symbolic figures and events to interpret and evaluate the historical.

Both within our traditions and in our dialogues with those of other traditions, such story telling and hearing involves intensive exercises of the imagination in which the elements of experience are rearranged in different configurations. The exercise threatens a certain kind of security and stability, and for that reason religious institutions have frequently tried to prevent contamination of this kind with other views and perspectives. Some Christian and other communities have tried to prevent their members from mixing with outsiders. For centuries the Catholic Church kept an index of forbidden books. Certain Orthodox Jewish communities have also tried to keep their young people from mixing with the Gentile world. These moves have all been based on the sense that there is a risk involved which is institutionally undesirable. But the resistance to hearing one another's stories also assumes that a religious commitment or understanding is something essentially static or complete. One can look at the matter quite differently and assume that it is in dialogue with others that we attain to a deeper understanding and commitment, and that a maturing faith is necessarily a changing one.

Besides the sharing of stories there is also a means of sharing ideals by participatory observation of rituals. It is no secret that many Christian communities have come to a new and deeper understanding not only of Judaism but of Christianity through participation in a Passover Seder, and it is evident that Jews who have invited Gentiles of Christian or other persuasion into their Passover Seder have grown into a larger sense of the liberation they celebrate with a view to its extension and fulfillment. A Catholic who participates in a Quaker meeting is likely to recognize a distinction but also a convergence of pneumatologies that breaks open wider horizons, while a Christian who is present at a Sikh communion is apt to grow not only in appreciation of the Sikhs and their ideals but also in perception of the fundamental meaning of the eucharist in the Christian tradition. The sharing of ritual is a powerful transcending of barriers because ritual is by its very nature a restructuring and focussing of the elements of experience so that they will be seen and known in a new light.

Perhaps the most obvious way to share ideals and visions is through a presentation and explanation of the codes of life and behavior that traditions have constructed for themselves. While in itself interesting and important, however, this is not really the best way to get to know the others because codes tend to establish boundaries rather than highlight the center. They tend to provide a safety net rather than a focus or a direction. Something similar may be said about the institutional structures: to know the hierarchic or organizational patterns of any of the Christian churches is to know very little about the people who make up those churches. Life indeed always structures itself, but structures do not beget life, so that their function and their significance remain at all times strictly subsidiary and peripheral. Something more may, however, be said for the official theologies of particular traditions where such theologies exist. The official theology is a kind of precipitate or crystallization of what has been going on in the tradition, and so, though in a less hardened state, are all the theologies that wrestle within a tradition trying to give it sharper definition. It is certainly very useful in dialogue between traditions to offer a presentation and explanation of theologies from one's own group and to listen and try to follow presentations and explanations of theologies from the other group.

Nevertheless, the exchange of theologies is not the fundamental or primary path to mutual understanding, but depends very heavily on some prior experience of the ritual, the life and the story. As Hans Gadamer has so incisively shown (*Truth and Method*, London: Sheed and Ward 1979), the meaning of a dance is in the dancing of it, the meaning of a song in the singing, and the meaning of a life in the living. One approaches the meaning of others' dances, songs and lives across bridges of empathy in which the imagination enters into experience other than its own. It is only at a third and intrinsically derivative level that explanations, theories and prescriptions can convey any meaning at all. In practical experience, interfaith and even interdenominational dialogue has often suffered in the past from institutional anxieties that prevented participants from entering the traditions of the other at the first and even at the second level, putting the derivative knowledge of the third level first. What this yields is an artificial and brittle type of understanding. That this has happened so much may be due in part to a widespread misunderstanding of the way people assimilate their own tradition as they grow up in it. In our scholastically and literarily inclined society we often proceed as though abstract ideas come first and are then applied and implemented, as though people primarily learn a theory and secondarily apply it in action. Such a conception tends to lend the theoretical account an importance and a permanence which is not really appropriate. It is not surprising that ecumenical initiatives based on such understanding tend to bear fruit in nothing more than additional books.

From what has been written above, it follows that Christians as such have a need to enter into dialogue. Particular denominations must do so with one another, inasmuch as they claim to be the *ekklesia* or gathering of God's people and because (with few exceptions) they claim the salvific will of God to be universal. There is an acknowledgment of solidarity in creation and in destiny, a solidarity in sin and in redemption. This alone should call for continuous dialogue to search for what is common and to consider what is alternate or complementary in understanding and experiencing the good news of salvation. This applies in a special way to Catholics because the Catholic tradition is characteristically based on the understanding of the redemption as a corporate project, on the importance of the sacramental principle (which concretizes religious experience), on the continuity of faith and reason which grounds the possibility of wider dialogue, on the understanding that grace makes the reconstruction of the world of human affairs possible, and on the conviction that the church of Jesus Christ cannot be in any way élitist. All of this suggests the immediate necessity of continuing dialogue among all those who call themselves Christian.

It is also true, however, and for many of the same reasons, that dialogue outside the ranks of Christians is a necessity. This wider ecumenism is something other than a simple missionary drive to invite others into the Christian persuasion. It is the need to know the others and to appreciate them as they are and for what they are. The conviction of the universal salvific will of God could be thought to require frantic efforts to convert others and to explain why, after all these centuries, so few of the peoples of the earth have become and remained Christian. But the same conviction could lead to a very different attitude; it could suggest that there are many paths of salvation, many ways of naming and worshipping the same ultimate, transcendent reality, many languages and rituals by which peoples search for communion with the divine and respond to the outreach of the divine in creation. If there are many such ways, then it is of overwhelming interest to know more about them, to see what we as Christians can learn from them, and to offer them a respectful exchange of all that makes up our faith-tradition and theirs.

Such exchanges are based, of course, on the understanding that the divine always transcends our comprehension and expression, so that the best that any of us can say is partial and figurative, not excluding the truth of what others have to say. It is based also on the conviction that we have a common starting point in human experience and a common end in the transcendent ultimate. That is to say: inter-religious dialogue is based on an act of faith that reality is not absurd, and that therefore what is truly ultimate is unified so that all quests for communion with the ultimate are in process of converging. It is not only a matter of courtesy, strategy or convention to respect what others have to say; it is an essential component of our own quest for truth.

To all of this the objection might be raised that the Christian churches as a whole, and the Catholic Church in particular, have commonly made claims directly in opposition to such open attitudes. The claim that there is one name under heaven by which all must be saved, that the cross of Jesus Christ is the universal means of salvation, that Jesus is a unique incarnation of the divine, that the revelation claimed by Christians gives definitive access to the divine, and even that other people of good faith are "anonymously Christian"

– all this seems incompatible with the kind of dialogue that has been described and proposed here. This is even more pressing in the case of Catholic doctrine, which has made similar claims of exclusivity and definitive access to truth, not only for what is written in Scripture but also for many formulations made in the course of Christian history by councils, or custom, or latterly by Rome.

There seem to be several ways of answering this. One way is to admit that such exclusivist claims have been made, but to declare them simply in error. There is a simplicity about this which is appealing. The disadvantage is that it is very difficult to find a convincing justification for claiming authority to stand above the tradition and judge it, or even to stand above the accepted authorities in the tradition and judge them in the name of the tradition itself. This kind of approach usually necessitates a sharp break, causing a schism within the community itself, as in the sixteenth-century Reformation. Moreover, as the Reformation shows, this is usually not a single split between a conservative faction holding to the old and a progressive faction moving to the new; it tends rather to be a split into many different factions each claiming some higher authority for reinterpreting the traditional positions in some particular way. As an approach to dialogue this is very indirect, because it begins with an argument that takes a long time to soften into amicable conversation within the tradition before there can be any conversation with those outside the tradition that is other than individual or factional.

There is another way to answer the objection. This is to see the exclusivist claims as part of a history in which the community of faith tried to establish its identity and had to differentiate itself from others before coming into any kind of conversation with them. This is a not uncommon human experience. Even sexual differentiation tends to happen somewhat along those lines: boys go through a stage of proving they are not "sissies," of not wanting to play with girls or even to acknowledge that they exist, and something similar happens with girls, while parents are likely to reflect how different things will be ten years later. The analogy may be weak, but it is there. An even stronger comparison may be made with patriotism which, for the immature of all ages, tends to involve a certain contempt and even hatred for people of other nations, but for the humanly and civically mature represents an established identity from which friendly dialogue and collaboration can be carried on. This has its possibilities when applied to the actual history of Christianity and of particular churches. In times of persecution or of threatened schism there is more tendency to be dogmatically rigid. The tendency can be noted, for instance, in post-Tridentine Catholicism and in the churches that existed behind the Iron Curtain. With this answer to the problem of exclusivity it would be necessary to show the context that makes self-definition so urgent and desperate, and to show also precedents in the tradition, or subsequent developments in the tradition, that make it possible to go beyond the more rigid interpretations.

There is a third way of responding to exclusivist claims – a way that is far more laborious but also more convincing within the faith-community of that tradition. This way is to take particular texts and subject them to an exegetical, hermeneutic and contextual study, to discover what questions they were answering within their own historical, linguistic and cultural setting. In many cases the answer is surprising because texts have been quoted mindlessly out of context in ways that have distorted their original meaning. A particularly interesting example of this is the claim, "Whoever wishes to be saved must first of all hold the Catholic faith, for anyone who does not maintain this whole and inviolate will surely be lost eternally."

This rather astonishing claim appears first at the beginning of the so-called Athanasian Creed, and after a lengthy and involved explanation of the Nicene faith, focussing on the triune perception of God and on the Incarnation, is reiterated by way of concluding the same creed: "This is the Catholic faith, and if anyone shall not faithfully and firmly believe it, he cannot be saved." The text takes on some importance because it became part of the liturgy of the hours in the mediaeval period and found a place in the Book of Common Prayer of the Anglican Church, as well as in modern Catholic worship each Sunday until the Second Vatican Council. Moreover, the formula is significant because it recurs in the Tridentine Profession of Faith, set out by Pope Paul IV in 1564, and demanded by the Council of Trent of all church dignitaries. In this setting it covers a far more detailed account of Christian beliefs including many points developed well after the ancient ecumenical councils. The exact statement here is: "This true Catholic belief without which no one can be saved . . . I promise . . . to hold and confess entire and undefiled . . ."

Taken out of context, this statement clearly means that there is no salvation for non-Christians, nor for Arians, Nestorians or Monophysites, nor (in the reiteration of the Tridentine Creed) for Protestants or Orthodox Christians. Faced with the horror of this truly vast *massa damnata*, Catholics are obviously under urgent constraint to take another careful look at this remarkable declaration. Strangely enough, in view of the influence it has had, we do not know the origin of the Athanasian Creed in which the exclusionary formula first appeared. It is known that it was not in fact composed by St Athanasius but was given his name because of its concern with Nicene orthodoxy and with the doctrines of Trinity and Incarnation. What appears far more likely is that it was written in Latin, probably in the early sixth century, and most likely in the church of Arles at a time when that church was threatened by the western Arians. Composed in a lovely sing-song pattern, it summarizes the trinitarian teaching of Augustine of Hippo, who was certainly seen as the champion of doctrinal orthodoxy in troubled times.

Given this context, it is immediately apparent that the author and the church in which the creed was first recited did not have non-Christians in mind at all in their exclusionary statements. Their obvious intent was to reinforce the knowledge and the confession of the traditional trinitarian teaching among their own church members – it is thought, primarily among the clergy who had to be forewarned about the errors which were being diffused. In this case, therefore, the apparent declaration that outsiders cannot be saved is really a declaration that insiders who let themselves be seduced from the mainline church are being drawn away from the source and channel of redemption which is the church of Jesus Christ and not any self-appointed group that may come in to divide and trouble the community with new teachings and arguments.

It is thought that the mediaeval fascination with this creed had less to do with concerns about the Arians, or even concerns about orthodoxy in general, than with the way this creed lends itself to choral recitation, the way it spells out a good deal of traditional doctrine, and the fact that it summarizes the teaching of St Augustine. There is no doubt that it reinforced some very exclusivist conceptions of salvation, but this does not seem to have been its intent either in its origins or in its mediaeval adoption into the liturgy. Moreover, the taking over of the exclusionary sentence by the creed of Trent seems to have had a purpose similar to the original purpose of the sentence in the creed *Quicunque*. A profession of faith was being required of those in positions of responsibility in the Catholic Church because of the great fear that they would be "seduced" unwittingly by the teachings of the Reformers. In that context, the profession of faith insists that it is the only true one, the only salvific one, as a warning not to be led astray. Again, the focus of attention is not on the outsiders but on the insiders who might be tempted away.

This still leaves a claim of superiority and implies that a move from the teachings of the Catholic faith (whether understood as the Nicene or as the post-Reformation Roman Catholic) is quite simply a move into error, and a catastrophic one. This in itself is not a position most conducive to open dialogue. However, it is not nearly as dogmatically exclusive of all others from the possibility of salvation as would appear from the statement taken out of context. To the narrower claim it may be said that as a general rule it is almost tautologous, that any tradition will claim fidelity from its members and see their departure as tragedy and betrayal. Because the concern of Christian churches is salvation, it is not altogether surprising that a church should say in its official accounts of itself, "If you leave me, you are leaving the means of salvation behind." But this kind of statement can be true in one sense and untrue in another. It is clearly true that means of salvation are being left behind. It is less evident that there are no other means of salvation to be found elsewhere. The intent to say the first may easily become a statement that implies the second interpretation.

It must also be said, in conclusion, that one who is not simply unfaithful from self-interest or unconcern, but who leaves because it is the next step in a serious search for the transcendent that has unfolded in that person's life, will have so strong a conviction from experience that any proclamation of exclusion from salvation will be unlikely to shake that person's resolution or convictions. Likewise, anyone who has found faith and communion in another tradition is unlikely to be personally troubled by assertions from particular Christian creeds that salvation is not to be found outside certain beliefs and loyalties proclaimed by those creeds. Yet for dialogue to be full and open it is certainly necessary to confront such exclusionary statements and strip them of exaggerated claims.

A Dialogue on Dialogue

—

Leonard Swidler

I. What dialogue means

When we speak of dialogue between religions or ideologies today we mean something rather definite, namely, a two-way communication between persons; one-way lecturing or speaking is obviously not meant by it. But there are many different kinds of two-way communication: fighting, wrangling, debating, etc. Clearly none of these is meant by dialogue. On the other extreme is the communication between persons who hold precisely the same views on a subject. This also we do not mean by dialogue; rather, we might call that something like encouragement, reinforcement – but certainly not dialogue. If we look at these two opposite kinds of two-way communication which are *not* meant by the word dialogue, we can learn quite precisely what we do in fact mean by the term dialogue.

To take the last example first, the principle underlying "reinforcement," etc. is the assumption that both sides have a total grasp on the truth of the subject and hence simply need to be supported in their commitment to it. Since the example, and its principle, are excluded from the meaning of dialogue, clearly dialogue must include the notion that neither side has a total grasp of the truth of the subject, but that both need to seek further. Secondly, the principle underlying "debating," etc. is the assumption that one side has all the truth concerning the subject and that the other side needs to be informed or persuaded of it. Since that example also, and its principle, are excluded from the meaning of dialogue, it is clearly implied that dialogue means neither side has a monopoly on the truth on the subject, but both need to seek further.

Now, it may turn out in some instances that after a more or less extensive dialogue it is learned that the two sides in fact agree completely on the subject discussed. Such a discovery, of course, does not mean that the encounter was a non-dialogue, but rather that the dialogue was the means of learning the new truth that both sides agreed on the subject; to continue from that point on, however, to speak only about the area of agreement would then be to move from dialogue to reinforcement.

To express the meaning of dialogue positively, then: dialogue is a two-way communication between persons who hold significantly differing views on a subject with the purpose of learning more truth about the subject from the other.

Such an analysis may to some seem obvious, and, hence, superfluous. But I think not. The term dialogue has become faddish, and is sometimes, like charity, used to cover a multitude of sins. For example, it is sometimes used by those who are quite convinced that they have all the truth on a subject, but feel that in today's climate, with "dialogue" in vogue, a less aggressive style will be more effective in communicating to the ignorant the truth that they already possess in full. Hence, while their encounters with others still rely on the older non-dialogue principle – that they have all the truth on a subject – their less importuning approach will now be *called* "dialogue." Such a use would appear to be merely an opportunistic manipulation of the term dialogue.

Perhaps some of those people, however, truly believe that they are engaging in dialogue when they employ such a "soft sell" approach and encourage their interlocutors also to express their own views on the subject – even though it is known ahead of time, of course, that they are false – for such a "dialogue" may well make the ignorant person more open to receiving the truth which the one side knows it already has. In that case, the "truth-holders" simply had a basic misunderstanding of the term dialogue and mistakenly termed their "convert-making" dialogue. Hence, the above clarification is important.

In this context, of course, we are speaking about a particular kind of dialogue, namely, interreligious dialogue in the broadest sense, that is, dialogue on a religious subject by persons who understand themselves to be in different religious traditions and communities. If religion is understood as an "explanation of the ultimate meaning of life and how to live accordingly," then that would include all such systems, even though they customarily would not be called religions but perhaps ideologies, such as atheistic humanism and Marxism; hence it is more accurate to speak of both interreligious and interideological dialogue.

II. Why dialogue arose

While one can justifiably point to a number of recent developments that have contributed to the rise of dialogue – e.g., growth in mass education, communications and travel, a world economy, threatening global destruction – a major underlying cause is a paradigm-shift in the West in how we perceive and describe the world. A paradigm is the model, the cluster of assumptions, on the basis of which phenomena are perceived and explained: for example, the geocentric paradigm for explaining the movements of the planets; a shift to another paradigm – as to the heliocentric – will have a major impact. Such a paradigm-shift occurred in the Western understanding of truth-statements which has made dialogue not only possible but even necessary.

Whereas the notion of truth in the West was largely absolute, static, monologic or exclusive up to the last century, it has subsequently become deabsolutized, dynamic and dialogic – in a word: relational. This "new" view of truth came about in at least six different but closely related ways.

Before the nineteenth century in Europe truth, that is, a statement about reality, was conceived in an absolute, static, exclusivistic "either-or" manner. It was thought that if a statement was true at one time, it was always true, and this applied not only to statements about empirical facts but also to statements about the meaning of things. This is a *classicist* or *absolutist* view of truth.

1. In the nineteenth century scholars came to perceive all statements about the truth of the meaning of something as being partially products of their historical circumstances; only by placing truth-statements in their historical situations, their historical *Sitz im Leben*, could they be properly understood. A text could be understood only in context. Hence, all statements about the meaning of things were seen to be deabsolutized in terms of time. This is a *historical* view of truth.

2. Later it was noted that we ask questions so as to obtain knowledge, truth, according to which we want to live; this is a *praxis* or *intentional* view of truth, that is, a statement has to be understood in relationship to the action-oriented intention of the thinker.

3. Early in this century Karl Mannheim developed what he called the sociology of knowledge, which points out that every statement about the truth of the meaning of something is perspectival, for all reality is perceived, and spoken of, from the cultural, class, sexual, and so forth perspective of the perceiver. This is a *perspectival* view of truth.

4. Ludwig Wittgenstein and many other thinkers have discovered something of the limitations of human language: every description of reality is necessarily only partial, for although reality can be seen from an almost limitless number of perspectives, human language can express things from only one perspective at once. This partialness and limitedness of all language is necessarily greatly intensified when one attempts to speak of the Transcendent, which by definition "goes-beyond." This is a *language-limited* view of truth.

5. The contemporary science of hermeneutics stresses that all knowledge is interpreted knowledge. That means that in all knowledge *I* come to know something; the object comes into me in a certain way, namely, through the lens that I use to perceive it. As Thomas Aquinas said, "Things known are in the knower according to the mode of the knower." This is an *interpretative* view of truth.

6. Still further, reality can "speak" to me only with the language that I give it. The "answers" that I receive back from reality will always be in the language, the thought-categories, of the questions I put to it. If the answers I receive are sometimes confused and unsatisfying, then I probably need to learn to speak a more appropriate language when I put questions to reality. If, for example, I ask the question, "How far is yellow?" of course I will receive a non-sense answer. Or if I ask questions about living things in mechanical categories, I will receive confusing and unsatisfying answers. So too will I receive confusing and unsatisfying answers to questions about human sexuality if I use categories that are solely physical-biological. Witness the absurdity of the answer that birth control is forbidden by the natural law: the question falsely assumes that the nature of humanity is merely physical-biological. This understanding of truth is a *dialogic* understanding.

In short, our understanding of truth and reality has been undergoing a radical shift. This new paradigm which is being born understands all statements about reality, especially about the meaning of things, to be historical, praxial or intentional, perspectival, language-limited or partial, interpretive, and dialogic. In short, our understanding of truth statements has become "deabsolutized" – it has become "relational." That is, all statements about reality are now seen to be *related* to the historical context, praxis intentionality, perspective, etc. of the speaker, and in that sense no longer "absolute." Hence, if my perception and description of the world is true only in a limited sense, that is, only as seen from my place in the world, then if I wish to expand my grasp of reality I need to learn from others what they know of reality that they can perceive from their place in the world that I cannot see from mine. That can happen only through dialogue.

III. Who should dialogue

An important question is, who can, who should, engage in interreligious, interideological dialogue? Clearly there is a fundamental communal aspect to such a dialogue. If a person is, for example, neither a Lutheran or a Jew, s/he could not engage in a specifically Lutheran-Jewish dialogue. Similarly, persons not belonging to any religious or ideological community could not, of course, engage in interreligious, interideological dialogue. They might very well engage in meaningful religious, ideological dialogue, but it simply would not be inter-religious, inter-ideological: between religions or ideologies.

Who, then, qualifies as a member of a religious community? If one is speaking of the official representation of a community at a dialogue, then the clear answer is those who are appointed by the appropriate official body in that community: the congregation, Bet Din, roshi, bishop, Central Committee or whatever. If it is not a case of official representation, then general reputation usually is looked to. However, some persons' qualifications can be challenged by elements within a community, even very important official elements. For example, the Vatican Congregation for the Doctrine of the Faith has declared that Professors Hans Küng and Charles Curran are no longer to be considered Catholic theologians. Now in both these cases hundreds of Catholic theologians subsequently stated publicly in writing that both these professors were indeed still Catholic theologians.

Ultimately, however, it seems best to follow the principle that each person should decide for her or himself whether or not they are members of a religious community. Extreme cases may at rare times present initial anomalies, but they will inevitably resolve themselves. Moreover, it is important to be aware that, especially in the initial stages of any interreligious, interideological dialogue, it is very likely that the literally ec-centric members of religious, ideological communities will be the ones who will have the interest and ability to enter into dialogue; the more centrist persons will do so only after the dialogue has been proved safe for the mainline, official elements to venture into.

It is likewise important to note that interreligious, interideological dialogue is not something to be limited to official representatives of communities. In fact, the great majority of the vast amount of such dialogue that has occurred throughout the world, particularly in the past three decades, has not been carried on by official representatives, although that too has been happening with increasing frequency.

What is needed is 1. an openness to learn from the other, 2. knowledge of one's own tradition, and 3. a similarly disposed and knowledgable dialogue partner from the other tradition. But this can happen on any level of knowledge and education. It is the openness to learn from the other that is the key. No one's knowledge of her/his own tradition can ever be complete; each person must continually learn more about it. One simply needs to realize that one's knowledge is in fact limited and know where to turn to gain the information needed. However, it is also important that the dialogue partners be more or less equal in knowledge of their own traditions, etc. The greater the asymmetry, the less the communication will be two-way, that is, dialogic.

Thus, it is important that interreligious, interideological dialogue *not* be limited to official representatives or even to the experts in the various traditions, although they both have their irreplaceable roles to play in the dialogue. Rather, dialogue should involve every level of the religious, ideological communities, all the way down to the "persons in the pews." Only thus will the religious, ideological communities learn from each other and come to understand each other as they truly are.

This insight was expressed very clearly and vigorously by the Catholic bishops of the world at Vatican II when the Council "exhorted *all the Catholic faithful* to recognize the signs of the times and to take an active and intelligent part in the work of ecumenism [dialogue among the Christian churches, and in an extended understanding, dialogue among the religions and ideologies, as is made clear by other Vatican II documents and the establishment of permanent Vatican Secretariats for dialogue with Non-Christians and with Non-Believers]." Not content with this exhortation, the bishops went on to say that, "in ecumenical work, [all] Catholics must . . . make the *first approaches* toward them [non-Catholics]." Just in case there were some opaque minds or recalcitrant wills out there, the bishops once more made it ringingly clear that ecumenism [interreligious, interideological dialogue] "involves the whole Church, faithful and clergy alike. It extends to everyone, according to the talent of each" (Vatican II, *Decree on Ecumenism*, 4,5). Surely this insight is not to be limited to the 800,000,000 Catholics in the world – and the further hundreds of millions they directly or indirectly influence – massive and important as that group may be.

What about the challenge, however, of those who charge that "dialogists" are really élitists because they define dialogue in such a "liberal" manner that only like-minded "liberals" can join in? Below I will argue in more detail that only those who have a "deabsolutized" understanding of truth will in fact be able to enter into dialogue. In other words, only those who understand all truth statements, that is, all statements about reality, to be always limited in a variety of ways, and in that sense not absolute, can enter into dialogue. However, this is no élitist discrimination against "absolutists," or fundamentalists, by not allowing them to engage in dialogue. Such a charge is simply another case of not understanding what dialogue is: a two-way communication so that both sides can learn. If one side grants that it has something to learn from the other, that admission presupposes that the first side has only a limited – a deabsolutized – grasp of truth concerning the subject. If one side thinks that it has an absolute grasp of the truth concerning the subject, it obviously believes that it has nothing to learn from the other side, and hence the encounter will not be a dialogue but some kind of attempt at one-way teaching or a debate. Thus the side with the absolutized view of truth will not only not be able to engage in dialogue, it will very much not want to – unless it falls into the category either of harboring the misunderstanding of the meaning of dialogue described earlier, or the intention of an opportunistic manipulation of the term.

IV. Kinds of dialogue

In the matter of what constitutes interreligious, interideological dialogue, it is important to notice that we normally mean a two-way communication in ideas and words. However, at times we give the term an extended meaning of joint action or collaboration and joint prayer or sharing of the spiritual or depth dimension of our tradition. Now while intellectual and verbal communication is indeed the primary meaning of dialogue, if the results from it do not spill over into the other two areas of action and spirituality, it will have proved sterile. More than that, it can lead toward a kind of schizophrenia and even hypocrisy.

On the positive side, serious engagement in joint action and/or spirituality will tend to challenge the previously-held intellectual positions and lead to dialogue in the cognitive field. For example, Catholic and Protestant clergy who found themselves together in Dachau concentration camp because of joint resistance to one or other Nazi anti-human action began to ask each other why they did what they did, and through dialogue were surprised to learn that they held many more positions in common than positions that separated them. In fact these encounters and others like them fostered the Una Sancta Movement in Germany, which in turn was the force that moved the Catholic Church in the Second Vatican Council (1962–65) officially to embrace ecumenism and interreligious dialogue after many centuries of vigorous official rejection.

Since religion is not something just of the "head" and the "hands," but also of the "heart" – of the whole human being – our encounter with our partner must also eventually include the depth or spiritual dimension. This spiritual dimension engages our emotions, our imagination, our intuitive consciousness. If we do not learn to know each other in this deepest dimension of our selves our dialogue will remain relatively superficial. Here the technique called by John Dunne "crossing over" can be of help. By it we focus on a central image, metaphor, from our partner's spiritual life and let it work on our imagination, our emotions, evoking whatever responses it may, leading us to different feelings. Then we return to our own inner world enriched, expanded, with a deeper sympathy for, and sensitivity to, our partner's inner world. Thereafter, within the context of this expanded inner dimension we will be prompted to look for new cognitive articulations adequate to reflect it, and we will be prompted to express our new awareness and understanding of our partner's religious reality in appropriate action.

Encountering our partner on only one or two levels will indeed be authentic dialogue, but, given the integrative and comprehensive nature of religion and ideology, it is only natural that we be led from dialogue on one level to the others. It is only with dialogue in this full fashion on all three levels that our interreligious, interideological dialogue will be complete.

V. Goals of dialogue

The general goal of dialogue can be said to be for each side to learn, and to change accordingly. Of course, if each side comes to the encounter primarily to learn from the other, then the other side must teach, and thus both learning and teaching occurs. However, we know that if each side comes to the encounter primarily to teach, both sides will tend to close up, and as a result neither teaching nor learning takes place.

In the dialogue we naturally gradually learn more and more about our partners and in the process shuck off the misinformation about them we may have had. But we also learn something more, something even closer to home.

Our dialogue partner also becomes for us something of a mirror in which we perceive our selves in ways we could not otherwise do. In the process of responding to the questions of our partners we look into our inner selves and into our traditions in ways that we perhaps never would otherwise, and thus come to know ourselves as we could not have done outside the dialogue. Further, in listening to our partners' descriptions of their perceptions of us we learn much about "how we are in the world." Since no one is simply in her or himself, but is always in relationship to others, "how we are in the world," how we relate to and impact on others, is in fact part of our reality, is part of us. For example, it is only by being in dialogue with another culture that we really come to know our own: I became aware of my particular American culture, for example, only as I lived in Europe for a number of years. It was in the mirror of my dialogue partner of European culture that I could become conscious of American culture as such with its similarities to and differences from European culture.

The expanded knowledge of ourselves and of the other that we gain in the dialogue cannot of course remain ineffective in our lives. As our self-understanding and understanding of those persons and those things around us change, so too must our attitude toward our selves and others change, and thus our behavior as well. Again, to the extent that this inner and outer change, this transformation, does not take place, we tend toward schizophrenia and hypocrisy. Whether one wants to speak of dialogue and then of the subsequent transformation as "beyond dialogue," as John Cobb does in his book *Beyond Dialogue*, or speak of transformation as an integral part of the continuing dialogue process, as Klaus Klostermaier does (*Journal of Ecumenical Studies*, 21.4, Fall 1984, pp. 755–9), need not detain us here. What is important to see is that the chain dialogue-knowledge-change must not be broken. If the final link, change, is not retained, the authenticity of the second, knowledge, and the first, dialogue are called into question. To repeat: the goal of dialogue is "for each side to learn, and change accordingly."

There are also communal goals in interreligious, interideological dialogue. Some of them will be peculiar to the situation of the particular dialogue partners. For example, several Christian churches may enter into dialogue with the goal of structural union in mind. Such union goals, however, will be something special to religious communities *within* one religion, that is, within Christianity, within Buddhism, within Islam, etc. However, dialogue *between* different religions and ideologies will not have this goal of structural union. Rather, it will seek first to know the dialogue partners as accurately as possible and try to understand them as sympathetically as possible. Dialogue will seek to learn what the partners have in common, and what their differences are.

There is a simple technique to follow in order to learn where the authentic commonalities and differences are between two religions or ideologies. Attempt to agree with the dialogue partner as far as possible on a subject without violating one's own integrity; where one can go no further, there is where the authentic difference is, and what has been shared up until that point are commonalities. Experience tells us that very often our true differences lie elsewhere than we had believed before the dialogue.

One communal goal in seeking to learn the commonalities and differences in two religions is to bridge over antipathies and misunderstandings – to draw closer together in thought, feeling and action on the basis of common features. However, this goal can be reached only if another principle is also observed. Interreligious, interideological dialogue must be a two-sided dialogue: beyond the community, and within it. We must be in regular dialogue with our fellow religionists, sharing with them the results of our interreligious, interideological dialogue so they too can enhance their understanding of what is held in common and where the differences truly are, for only thus can the whole communities grow in knowledge and inner and outer transformation, and thereby bridge over antipathies and draw closer. In fact, if this two-sided dialogue is not maintained, the individual dialogue partners alone will grow in knowledge and consequently be changed, thus slowly moving away from their unchanging community and becoming a third reality, a *tertium quid* – hardly the intended integrative goal of dialogue.

It is obvious that it is important to learn as fully as possible the things we share in common with our dialogue partners, which most often will be much more extensive than we could have anticipated beforehand; we will thus be drawn together in greater harmony. However, it is likewise important that we learn more comprehensively what our differences are. These differences may be: 1. complementary, as for example a stress on the prophetic rather than the mystical; 2. analogous, as for example, the notion of God in the Semitic religions and of *sunyata* in Mahayana Buddhism; or 3. contradictory, where the acceptance of one entails the rejection of the other, as for example, the Judeo-Christian notion of the inviolable dignity of each individual person and the now largely disappeared Hindu custom of *suttee*, widow-burning. The matter of the third category of differences will be discussed below, but here we can note that the differences in the first two categories are not simply to be perceived and acknowledged; they should in fact be cherished and celebrated both for their own sakes and because by discerning them we have extended our own understanding of reality, and of how to live accordingly – the main goal of dialogue.

VI. The means of dialogue

A wide variety of means and techniques of dialogue have been successfully used, and doubtless some are yet to be developed. The overall guiding principle in this matter, however, should be, 1. to use our creative imaginations and our sensitivity for persons. Techniques already utilized range from joint lectures and dialogues by experts from different traditions that are listened to by large audiences on one extreme, to personal conversations between "rank and file" individuals from different traditions on the other. An important rule to keep in mind, however, whenever something more formal than the personal conversation is planned is that, 2. all the traditions to be engaged in a dialogue should be involved in its initial planning. This is especially true when different communities first begin to encounter each other. Then dialogue on the potential dialogue becomes an essential part of the dialogic encounter.

Clearly in the first encounters between communities, 3. the most difficult points of differences should not be tackled. Rather, those subjects which give promise of highlighting commonalities should be treated so that mutual trust between the partners can be established and developed. For without mutual trust there will be no dialogue.

Essential to the development of this needed mutual trust is that, 4. each partner should come to the dialogue with total sincerity and honesty. In dialogue my partners wish to learn to know me and my tradition as we truly are; this is impossible, however, if I am not totally sincere and honest. The same is true for my partners, of course; I cannot learn to know them and their traditions truly if they are not completely sincere and honest. Note also, that we must simultaneously presume total sincerity and honesty in our partners as well as practice them ourselves, otherwise there will be no trust – and without trust there will be no dialogue.

In dialogue care must also be taken, 5. to compare our ideals with our partner's ideals and our practices with our partner's practices. If we compare our ideals with our partner's practices we will always "win," but of course we will learn nothing – a total defeat of the purpose of dialogue.

Mention has already been made earlier of several other "means" of dialogue 6. Each partner in the dialogue must define her- or himself; only a Muslim, for example, can know from the inside what it means to be a Muslim, and this self-understanding will change, grow, expand, deepen as the dialogue develops, and hence perforce can be accurately described only by the one experiencing the living, growing religious reality. 7. Each partner should come to the dialogue with no fixed assumptions as to where the authentic differences between the traditions are; only after following the partner with sympathy and agreement as far as one can without violating one's own integrity will the true point of difference be determined. 8. Only equals can engage in full authentic dialogue; the degree of inequality will determine the degree of two-way communication, that is, the degree of dialogue experienced.

A major means of dialogue is 9. a self-critical attitude toward ourself and our tradition. If we are not willing to take a self-critical look at our own, and *our tradition's*, position on a subject, the implication clearly is that we have nothing to learn from our partner – but if that is the case we are not interested in dialogue, the primary purpose of which is to learn from our partner. To be sure, we come to the dialogue as a Buddhist, as a Christian, as a Marxist, etc., with sincerity, honesty and integrity. However, self-criticism does not mean a lack of sincerity, honesty, integrity. In fact, a lack of self-criticism will mean there is no valid sincerity, no true honesty, no authentic integrity.

In the end the most fundamental means to dialogue is, 10. having a correct understanding of dialogue, which is *a two-way communication so that both partners can learn from each other, and change accordingly*. If this basic goal is kept firmly in view and acted on with imagination, then creative, fruitful dialogue, and a growing transformation of each participant's life and that of their communities, will follow.

VII. The subject of dialogue

We already spoke about choosing first those subjects which promise to yield a high degree of common ground so as to establish and develop mutual trust, and the three main areas of dialogue: the cognitive, active and spiritual.

In some ways the latter, the spiritual area, appears to be the most attractive, at least to those with a more interior, mystical, psychological bent. Moreover, it promises a very large degree of commonality: the mystics appear to all meet together on a high level of unity with the Ultimate Reality, no matter how it is described, including even in the more philosophical systems, e.g., Neoplatonism. The greatest of the Muslim Sufis, Jewish Kabbalists, Hindu Bhaktas, Christian mystics, Buddhist Bodhisattvas and Platonist philosophers, for instance, all seem to be at one in their striving for and experience of unity with the One, which in the West is called God, *Theos*. Sometimes the image is projected of God being the peak of the mountain that all humans are climbing by way of different paths. Each has a different way (*hodos* in Christian Greek; *halachah* in Jewish Hebrew; *shar'ia* in Muslim Arabic; *marga* in Hindu Sanskrit; *magga* in Buddhist Pali; *tao* in Chinese Taoism) to reach *Theos*, but all are centered on the one goal. Hence, such an interpretation of religion or ideology is called theocentric.

Attractive as theocentrism is, one must be cautious not to wave the varying understandings of God aside as if they were totally without importance; they can make a significant difference in human self-understanding, and hence in how we behave toward ourselves, each other, the world around us, and the Ultimate Source. Furthermore, a theocentric approach has the disadvantage of not including non-theists in the dialogue. This would exclude not only atheistic humanists and Marxists, but also nontheistic Theravada Buddhists, who do not deny the existence of God but rather understand ultimate reality in a non-theistic, non-personal manner (theism posits a "personal" God, *Theos*). An alternative way to include these partners in the dialogue even in this area of "spirituality" is to speak of the search for ultimate meaning in life, for "salvation" (*salus* in Latin, meaning a salutary, whole, holy life; similarly, *soteria* in Greek), as what all humans have in common in the "spiritual" area, theists and non-theists. Hence, we can speak of a soteriocentrism.

In the active area dialogue needs to take place in a fundamental way on the underlying principles for action which motivate each tradition. Again, many similarities will be found, but also differences which will prove significant in determining the communities' differing stands on various issues of personal and social ethics. Only by carefully and sensitively locating those underlying ethical principles for ethical decision-making can later misunderstandings and unwarranted frustrations in specific ethical issues be avoided. Then particular ethical matters, such as sexual ethics, social ethics, ecological ethics, medical ethics, can become the focus of interreligious, interideological dialogue – and ultimately joint action where it has been found congruent with each tradition's principles and warranted in the concrete circumstances.

It is in the cognitive area where the range of possible subjects is greatest. It is practically unlimited – remembering the caution that the less difficult topics be chosen first and the more difficult later. That having been said, however, every dialogue group should be encouraged to follow creatively its own inner instinct and interests. Some groups will start with more particular, concrete matters and then be drawn gradually to discuss the underlying issues and principles. Others will begin with more fundamental matters and eventually will be drawn to reflect on more and more concrete implications of the basic principles already discovered. In any case, if proper preparation and sensitivity are provided for, no subject should *a priori* be declared off-limits.

Here we can draw encouragement from what may be for some perhaps an unexpected source, the Vatican Curia. The Secretariat for Dialogue with Unbelievers stated that even "doctrinal dialogue should be initiated with courage and sincerity, with the greatest freedom and with reverence." It then went on to make a statement that is quite amazing in its liberality: "Doctrinal discussion requires perceptiveness, both in honestly setting out one's own opinion and in recognizing the truth everywhere, *even if the truth demolishes one so that one is forced to reconsider one's own position, in theory and in practice, at least in part.*" The Secretariat then insisted that "in discussion the truth will prevail by no other means than by the truth itself. Therefore the liberty of the participants must be ensured by law and reverenced in practice" (Secretariatus pro Non-credenti, *Humane personae dignitatem*, 28 August 1968). These are strong words – which again should be applicable not only to the Catholics of the world, but in general.

VIII. When to dialogue – and when not

In principle we ought to be open to dialogue with all possible partners on all possible subjects. This principle should normally be followed today and doubtless for many years to come because the world's religions and ideologies have stored up so much misinformation about and hostility toward each other that it is almost impossible for us to know ahead of time what our potential partner is truly like on any given subject. Hence, we normally need first of all to enter into sincere dialogue with every potential partner, at least until we learn where our true differences lie.

1. Kinds of authentic differences

In this question of differences, however, we have to be very careful in the distinctions we need to make. As outlined above, in the process of the dialogue we will often learn that what we thought were real differences were in fact only apparent: different words or misunderstandings merely hid commonly shared positions. However, when we enter dialogue we have to allow for the possibility that we will ultimately learn that on some matters we will find not a commonality but an authentic difference. As mentioned above, these authentic differences can be of three kinds: complementary, analogous or contradictory. Complementary authentic differences will indeed be true differences, but not such that only one could be valid. Furthermore, our experience tells us that the complementary differences will usually far outnumber the contradictory ones. Likewise, learning of these authentic but complementary differences will not only enhance one's knowledge but also may very well lead to the desire to adapt one or more of the partners' complementary differences for oneself. For as the very term indicates, the differences somehow complete each other, as the Chinese Taoist saying puts it: "Xiang fan xiang cheng" (contraries complete each other).

Just as we must always be extremely cautious about "placing" our differences *a priori*, lest in acting precipitously we misplace them, so too, we must not too easily and quickly place our true differences in the contradictory category. For example, perhaps Hindu *moksha*, Zen Buddhist *satori*, Christian "freedom of the children of God," and Marxist "communist state" could be understood as different, but nevertheless analogous, descriptions of true human liberation. In speaking here of true but analogous differences in beliefs or values, we are no longer talking about discerning teachings or practices in our partner's tradition which we might then wish to appropriate for our own tradition. That indeed does and should happen, but then we are speaking of something which either the two traditions ultimately hold in common and was perhaps atrophied or suppressed in one, or is an authentic but complementary difference. However, if this difference is perceived as analogous rather than complementary or contradictory, it will be seen to operate within the total organic structure of the other religion-ideology and to fulfill its function properly only within it. It could not have the same function, i.e., relationship to the other parts, in our total organic structure, and hence would not be understood to be in direct opposition, in contradiction to the "differing" element within our structure. At the same time it needs to be remembered that these real but analogous differences in beliefs or values should be seen not as in conflict with one another, but as parallel in function, and in that sense analogous.

Still, at times we can find contradictory truth claims, value claims, presented by different religious-ideological traditions. That happens only when they cannot be seen as somehow ultimately different expressions of the same thing (a commonality) or as complementary or analogous. But when it happens, even though it be relatively rare, a profound and unavoidable problem faces the two communities. What should be their attitude and behavior toward each other? Should they remain in dialogue, tolerate each other, ignore each other, or oppose each other? The problem is especially pressing in matters of value judgments. For example, what should the Christian (or Jew, Muslim, Marxist) have done in face of the now largely, but unfortunately not entirely, suppressed Hindu tradition of widow-burning (*suttee*)? Try to learn its value, tolerate it, ignore it, oppose it (in what manner?). Or the Nazi ideology's tenet of killing all Jews? These are relatively clear issues, but what of a religion-ideology that approves slavery, as Christianity, Judaism and Islam did until a century ago? Perhaps that is clear enough today, but what of sexism – or only a little sexism? Or the claim that only through capitalism – or socialism – human liberation can be gained? Deciding on the proper stance becomes less and less clear-cut.

It was eventually clear to most non-Hindus in the nineteenth century that the proper attitude was not dialogue with Hinduism on *suttee*, but opposition; but apparently it was not so clear to all non-Nazis that opposition to Jewish genocide was the right stance to take. Further, it took Christians almost two thousand years to come to that conclusion concerning slavery. Many religions and ideologies today stand in the midst of a battle over sexism, some even refusing to admit the existence of the issue. Finally, the controversial nature of the contemporary captialism-socialism issue needs no argument.

Clearly, important contradictory differences between religions or ideologies do exist and at times warrant not dialogue, but opposition. We also make critical judgments on the acceptability of positions within our own traditions and, rather frequently, within our personal lives. But surely this exercise of our critical faculties is not to be limited to ourselves and our tradition; this perhaps most human of faculties should be made available to all – with all the proper constraints and concerns for dialogue already detailed at length. It must first be determined on what grounds we can judge whether a religious or ideological difference is in fact contradictory, and then, if it is, whether it is of sufficient importance and a nature to warrant active opposition.

Since all religions and ideologies are attempts to explain the ultimate meaning of human life and how to live accordingly, it would seem that those doctrines and customs which are perceived as hostile to human life are not complementary or analogous but contradictory, and that opposition should be proportional to the extent they threaten life. What is to be included in an authentically full human life must then be the measure against which all elements of all religions or ideologies must be tested as we make judgments

about whether they are in harmony, complementarity, analogy or contradiction, and then act accordingly.

2. Full human life

Human
Rights

Because human beings are by nature historical beings, what it means to be
fully human is evolving. At basis everything human flows from what would
seem to be acceptable to all as a description of the minimally essential
human structure, that is, being an animal who can think abstractly and make
free decisions. Only gradually has humanity come to the contemporary
position where claims are made in favor of "human rights," that things are
due to all humans specifically because they are human. This position has
not been held always and everywhere. In fact, for the most part it was hardly
conceived until recently.

Only slightly over a hundred years ago, for example, slavery was still
widely accepted and even vigorously defended and practiced by high
Christian churchmen, not to speak of Jewish and Muslim slave traders. Yet
today this radical violation of "human rights" has largely been eliminated
both in practice and in law. No thinker or public leader would today
contemplate justifying slavery, at least under that name (see the 1948
United Nations Universal Declaration of Human Rights, article 4). Here is
an obvious example of the historical evolution of the understanding of what
it means to be fully human, i.e., that human beings are by nature radically
free.

What has been acknowledged fundamentally in this century as the
foundation of being human is that human beings ought to be autonomous in
their decisions – such decisions being directed by their own reason and
limited only by the same rights of others: "All human beings are born free
and equal in dignity and rights. They are endowed with reason and
conscience and should act toward one another in a spirit of brotherhood"
(Universal Declaration, article 1). This autonomy in the ethical sphere,
which Thomas Aquinas already recognized in the thirteenth century,[1]
expanded into the social, political spheres in the eighteenth century and is
well encapsulated in the slogan of the French Revolution, "Liberty, Equality, Fraternity" (contemporary consciousness of sexist language would
lead to a substitute like "Solidarity" for "Fraternity"). In the term "Liberty"
are understood all personal and civil rights; in the term "Equality" are
understood the political rights of participation in public decision-making; in
the term "Solidarity" are understood (in an expanded twentieth-century
sense) social rights.

The great religious communities of the world, though frequently resistant in the past, and too often still resistant in the present, have likewise
often and in a variety of ways expressed a growing awareness of and
commitment to many of the same notions of what it means to be fully
human. Thus through dialogue humanity is painfully slowly creeping

toward a consensus on what is involved in an authentically full human life. The 1948 United Nations Declaration of Human Rights was an important step in that direction. But, of course, much more consensus needs to be attained if interreligious, interideological dialogue is to reach its full potential.

IX. Christianity and dialogue

Earlier it was pointed out that the paradigm-shift in epistemology in the past hundred years has prepared the ground for dialogue and even made it necessary. This occurred first in the "West," but now the "West" is spreading over the globe, and so is the epistemological paradigm-shift and the consequent need for dialogue. Since Christianity has been at the heart of Western civilization, it could not escape this paradigm-shift and the move toward dialogue. It in fact had already undergone a radical paradigm-shift very early in its history, namely, the shift from perceiving and understanding reality in terms of the Semitic worldview to understanding it in terms of the Hellenistic worldview. This was a profound shift that occurred in the first centuries of Christian history, the magnitude of which has not been matched until the present era.

As the epistemological paradigm-shift began to gain ground in Christianity in the twentieth century – in a highly-visible institutional way in Catholicism with Vatican II (1962–65) – commitment to dialogue also spread, as was also dramatically reflected in Vatican II. As a consequence Christianity has been at the forefront of the promotion of dialogue among the world's religions and ideologies.

But what of the traditional Christian claim to be the exclusive and universal means of salvation? How can it be brought into a dialogue with other religions, which necessarily entails the assumption that Christianity does not have a complete, exclusive, absolute hold on the truth of salvation? More specifically, what of those statements in the New Testament and Christian tradition which stated such claims explicitly? Are they simply to be dismissed? Clearly not. They must be dealt with seriously.

X. A dialogue on salvation through the "divine" Christ

What exactly is meant by "salvation"? The word salvation has to a large extent been significantly altered in the Christian tradition from its meaning in Israelite religion and its root meaning in Greek and Latin. Since the third century AD it has for the most part been given a restricted meaning, namely, that when believers in Jesus Christ die, if they have remained faithful, they will go to heaven. Salvation here means being "saved" externally. But that is not at all what the word basically means. Its primary meaning is internal.

As noted earlier, in its Greek and Latin forms, "*soterion/soteria*" and "*salvatio*," "salvation," comes from the root "*sao*" in Greek and "*salus*" in Latin, meaning wholeness, health or wellbeing. The same is true of the Germanic root of the word, "*Heil*," which adjectivally also means whole, hale, healed, healthy. Indeed, this is also where the English word "holy" comes from. To be holy means to be whole, to lead a whole, a full life. When we lead a whole, full life, we are holy, we attain salvation, wholeness. Hence, one can attain salvation in a secondary, external sense, that is, be "saved," only by being returned to the integrated state of external and internal wholeness, salvation in the primary sense.

In any case, Christianity has traditionally claimed that salvation in whatever sense comes through God's exclusive self-revelation in the "divine" Christ; there is no other way to salvation because Jesus Christ alone is ontologically God in human form. This was made definitive in the ecumenical councils of the fourth and fifth centuries, culminating in Chalcedon in AD 451 but was claimed already to have been stated clearly in the New Testament as well. However, many contemporary Christian scholars argue that the latter claim is unwarranted. This is not the place to analyze all the possible texts in the New Testament, but it would be helpful to look at what is perhaps the major text put forward in support of this claim.

1. Logos theology

The Prologue to John's Gospel says, "In the beginning was the Word, and the Word was with God, and the Word was God . . . and the Word became flesh" (Jn 1:1,14). Keeping in mind that here we have a Jew writing largely for fellow Jews, it must be recalled that several figures and images were used in biblical and early Jewish writings as *literary images* of the invisible God as made perceivable to humans. There is the Spirit (*ruach*) of God, who already in Genesis 1:1 moves over the darkness in creation; Wisdom (*hokmah*), who is present at creation (Prov. 8:22f.; Ben Sira 24:9); God's Word, who in numerous biblical (*dabar*, Hebrew) and post-biblical (*memra*, Aramaic) texts expresses God to humanity, as also does God's *Torah* (Law) in both biblical and post-biblical texts; and God's Glory or Presence (*shekhinah*) in post-biblical Jewish material. It is within the context of this plethora of Jewish imagery of "God's visible side turned toward humanity" that John wrote and his Jewish readers understood him. But these were all literary metaphors, not ontological substances, and that was likewise true of John's *logos*, the Word (*dabar, memra*).

For the Jews, the Word of God was God speaking: God spoke and the world was created. The *Torah* was God's Word – indeed the Ten Commandments, the Deca-Logue, means God's "Ten Words." God spoke to Israel through the prophets for hundreds of years. In short, the whole Jewish experience of God was God speaking, expressing self, offering self for a relationship with human beings. "This self-expression of God had been going on for a long time before Jesus. It went back as far as humankind could remember. It seemed that God had always been speaking, from the beginning of the world."² Thus, as with Wisdom and the Spirit, it seemed to the Jews that the Word had been with God from the beginning, indeed, again like Wisdom and Spirit, was God as perceived by humanity; it "expressed God's own selfhood, and the one who encountered the word encountered God."³

And why did those ancient Jews see Jesus as God's Word become flesh? Because their experience of Jesus was that he was a diaphany of God: "everything God has ever said is summed up in Jesus. It is all said there, every word. Not only are the teachings of Moses and the prophets summarized in the teaching of Jesus; everything God wants to reveal about who God is is shown in who Jesus is for us." Furthermore, "Jesus is not just someone who has occasional words to say to us on God's behalf. He is in all the dimensions of his life God's self-revelation. Thus the word of God was enfleshed in a human life . . . This is the Johannine vision as scholars reconstruct it today."⁴

2. Dialogue suggests a resolution

I would like to call attention to a possible resolution to the seemingly intractable problem between Christians and non-Christians, and for the modern mind in general, over the Christian claim of the confluence of the human and the divine in Jesus, which has come out of interreligious dialogue – specifically the dialogue between Christianity and Buddhism.

As a result of his long dialogue with Buddhism, the Japanese Christian Katsumi Takizawa (1909–1984) distinguishes between what he terms the primary and the secondary contacts of God with the human self. The first contact is the unconditional fact that God is with each one of us, is the very ground of our selves. This "contact" is real even though we may be unaware of it. The second contact occurs when we are awakened to that primary fact, allowing "the self to live in conscious accord with the will of God."⁵

> According to Takizawa, Jesus was a man who was awakened to the primary fact – that is, he attained the secondary contact, and he did this so thoroughly and completely that he became a model for other selves . . . Jesus was the person who in Hebrew tradition played the same role as did Gautama Buddha in the Indian tradition. The ground of salvation is the primary contact of God with the self, and this is the common ground of both Buddhism and Christianity.⁶

Utilizing this distinction, another Japanese Christian, Seiichi Yagi, analyzes the "I" in the words of Jesus. He argues as follows: Jesus at times speaks in a way that clearly indicates the distinction between himself and God and at other times in a way that indicates a unity between him and God. This occurs in various places in the several Gospels, perhaps most clearly in John's Gospel. Jesus speaks of the unity between him and God, whom he calls the Father: "That all may be one as you Father in me and I in you . . . that they may be one as we are one, I in them and you in me" (Jn 17:21, 23); "Anyone who has seen me has seen the Father" (Jn 14:9); "Do you not believe that I am in the Father and the Father in me? The words I speak to you I do not speak of myself; but the Father who dwells in me does his works" (Jn 14:10). Here, when Jesus speaks it is fundamentally the Father speaking through him. The secondary contact has been so complete that it is the language of the unity between God the Father and Jesus that comes forth. And yet there is a distinction between them, for Jesus obeys the Father when he says: "For I have not spoken of myself; but the Father who sent me gave me a commandment, what I should say, and speak" (Jn 12:49).

> In John 14:10, Father and Son can be seen as two concentric circles in which the two centers, coincide, whereas in John 12:49, Father and Son appear as two centers in an ellipse, the latter obeying the former. . . . Christ is the Son of God insofar as the ultimate subject of the Son is the Father, but also insofar as the Father and the Son are distinguished from each other. They are paradoxically one.[7]

Yagi goes on to note that these two types of relationship between Jesus and God, the elliptic and the concentric, remind him of the two major kinds of Christologies in the ancient church, the Antiochene and the Alexandrian. The Antiochenes (elliptic) maintained that there were two centers in the person of Jesus, the divine and the human, and that the latter obeyed the former. The Alexandrians (concentric) insisted that both centers coincided. "The ancient church, therefore, maintained that both Christologies were true when, in the Council of Chalcedon, it declared that the divinity and the humanity of Christ were distinguishable but not separable."[8]

Such an explanation, I believe, makes sense out of the apparently conflicting language of the Gospels and helps to make the reality that paradoxical language points to available to a contemporary person; if the council of Chalcedon can be understood to be saying something similar it also helps to translate that Hellenistic ontological language into terms that likewise find resonance in a contemporary person's experience and thought patterns. It should be noticed, however, that Yagi's explanation is largely in psychological rather than abstract metaphysical terms. Further, what is said to be true in Jesus' case, that the secondary contact with God (enlightenment, *satori*) can in principle happen to every human being. Indeed, Jesus' language is full of exhortations to follow him, imitate him, be one with him and the Father.

Put in slightly different terms: Jesus was so completely open to all dimensions of reality, to all being – as all human beings are in principle – that he was totally suffused with an inpouring of being in a "radical" way which included the "Root" of all being, God. Thus he was thoroughly human because he was divine – through and through – which is evidenced in what he thought, taught and wrought.

XI. A dialogue on "divinization" in religions

The dialogue between Christianity and Buddhism has something further to teach us Christians in our understanding of our Christologies, and hence also about our relationship with non-Christians. The "divinization" of the historical Jesus into the "divine" Christ which occurred in Christianity as it moved from the Semitic cultural world into the Hellenistic world was matched by a similar development with the "divinization" of the historical Siddharta Gautama into the "divine" Buddha ("Buddha," like "Christ," is not a proper name but a title; it means "the enlightened one" and "Christ" means "the anointed one") as it moved from the Indian cultural world into the Chinese and Far Eastern world. Connected with this is the development from the "internal" understanding of "salvation" to the "external." This was like the movement from the "teaching Jesus" to the "proclaimed Christ," from the religion *of* Jesus to the religion *about* Jesus the Christ, from the "Jesus of history" to the "Christ of faith."

These shifts are also in many ways paralleled in Buddhism with the movement from the "internal" understanding of "salvation" (termed *jiriki*, "self-power," in Japanese) to the "external" understanding (*tariki*, "other power"), from the "teaching Gautama" to the "proclaimed Buddha," from the religion *of* Gautama to the religion *about* Gautama the Buddha, from "the Gautama of history" (*Shakyamuni*) to the "Buddha of belief" (*Maitreya Buddha* and *Amida Buddha*).

Seeing the same kind of developments occurring in such disparate religious cultures (one even being theistic and the other originally non-theistic) should make Christians ask themselves: What deeper grasping toward an underlying insight is represented by these "divinizing" movements? Perhaps one way to express this deeper insight is as follows.

For Christians, Jesus is the key figure through whom they get in touch with those dimensions of reality which go beyond, which transcend, the empirical, the everyday. This is fundamentally what Christologies are all about. All are attempts through the figure Jesus to come into contact with the transcendent, the "divine" – each Christology being perceived, conceived and expressed in its own cultural categories and images. Some do it better, even much better, than others; some do it badly. Naturally they are all culture-bound. Otherwise they would not reflect and effectively speak to the people in that culture. But of course concomitantly each Christology is proportionately limited in effectiveness in regard to other cultures, whether the cultural differences result from variations in geography, time, class, or whatever.

All Christians naturally can and should learn from the insights and failures of all other Christians' reaching out for the transcendent in their Christologies and other theological reflections, but what is "religiously specific" about Christians is that these Christologies, these theological reflections, are (or at least should be) intimately connected and compatible with the person Jesus of Nazareth – though of course they are not limited to imitating him in cultural detail.

Thus it should become clear to us Christians, and others, that in moving from talk about the "internal" to the "external," from the human to the divine, from Jesus to Christ, we, like the Buddhists and others, are attempting to express an experienced reality that transcends our everyday human experience, and hence also our everyday human language. We assert that there is a deeper reality which goes beyond the empirical surface experiences of our lives, and for us Jesus is the bond-bursting means of becoming aware of that deeper reality (as for Buddhists it is Gautama). For us Christians, it is pre-eminently in Jesus that we encounter the divine, and therefore we move to talk about the divine in Jesus. Hence our attempt to speak of the divine in Jesus, of Christ, etc., is not a mistake, but rather the result of the need to try to give expression to trans-empirical reality. At the same time, however, we must be aware that when we attempt to speak of the transcendent we will naturally have to use trans-empirical language, that is, metaphor, symbol and the like. The mistake we must be cautious to avoid in this situation is erroneously to think that when we speak about the transcendent we are using empirical language. We are not. We cannot. At the same time we must also be cautious to avoid being reductionist and erroneously thinking that all talk about the transcendent is merely fantasizing, that since Jesus was merely a human being, all later talk about the divine in him, etc., is simply romantic emoting with no referent in reality.

As I have argued, the move toward "divinization" is in fact a response to an experienced profound reality. It should not be dismissed, but held on to for the vital insight into the meaning of human life it strives for. However, it must be correctly understood for what it is, lest it become an idol, an image falsely adored, rather than the Reality toward which it points. When it is thus correctly understood and affirmed, we will then have reached what Paul Ricoeur calls the "second naiveté," that is, the state of awareness in which the affirmation of the symbol, understood correctly for what it is, further unlocks for us the deeper, trans-empirical reality.

If this line of thought, prompted by seeing the parallels in "divinization" in Christianity and Buddhism, has any validity in explaining how Christians are coming to understand their Christologies, then many of the disagreements between Christians and non-Christians in this area will disappear. Of course, this will not turn non-Christians into Christians, for them Jesus is not the door to the divine as he is for Christians, but perhaps it will dissipate their charges against Christians of idolatry or spinning fairy tales.

Thus, in summary, the reply to the question "what does the Christian do about all the Christian traditions and doctrines that speak of Jesus Christ as God, the second person of the Blessed Trinity?" must of course be that they are not to be just dismissed. However, they are also not to be merely repeated with no further reflection. Simply to parrot the past is to pervert it. They must be taken with utmost seriousness, analyzed for the kind of language they are and the reality they seek to express; they must be wrestled with and translated into our own contemporary thought-categories. This is a huge task which has only been begun – and I have offered a few suggestions for it here.

XII. Conclusion

The conclusion from these reflections is, I believe, clear: interreligious, interideological dialogue is absolutely necessary in our contemporary world. Every religion and ideology can again make its own several official statements from the Catholic Church about the necessity of dialogue, starting with Pope Paul VI in his first encyclical:

> Dialogue is demanded nowadays . . . It is demanded by the dynamic course of action which is changing the face of modern society. It is demanded by the pluralism of society, and by the maturity man has reached in this day and age. Be he religious or not, his secular education has enabled him to think and speak, and to conduct a dialogue with dignity (*Ecclesiam suam*, no. 78).

To this the Vatican Curia added:

> All Christians should do their best to promote dialogue between men of every class as a duty of fraternal charity suited to our progressive and adult age . . . The willingness to engage in dialogue is the measure and the strength of that general renewal which must be carried out in the Church [read: in every religion and ideology] (*Humanae personae dignitatem*, 28 August 1968, no. 1).

Notes

1. Thomas Aquinas, *Summa Theologiae*, I–II, Q. 91, a. 2: "*Inter cetera autem rationalis creatura excellentiori quodam modo divinae providentiae subiacet, inquantum et ipsa fit providentiae particeps, sibi ipsi et aliis providens.*"

2. Thomas N. Hart, *To Know and Follow Jesus*, New York: Paulist Press 1984, p. 98. Some additional contemporary scholars who treat the question of the divinity of Jesus in the New Testament are: Edward Schillebeeckx, *Jesus*, New York: Seabury Press and London: Collins 1979; Piet Schoonenberg, *The Christ*, New York: Seabury Press 1971; Piet Schoonenberg, "'He Emptied Himself': Philippians 2:7," in *Who Is Jesus of Nazareth?*, *Concilium* 11, New York: Paulist Press 1965, pp. 47–66; James D. G. Dunn, *Christology in the Making*, London: SCM Press and Philadelphia: Westminster Press 1980.

3. Hart, *Jesus*, p. 98.

4. Ibid., p. 99.

5. Seiichi Yagi, "'I' in the Words of Jesus," in Paul Knitter and John Hick, eds., *The Myth of Christian Uniqueness: Toward a Pluralistic Theology of Religions*, Maryknoll: Orbis Books and London: SCM Press 1987, p. 117. Yagi here summarizes this aspect of Takizawa's work and goes on to apply it to Jesus and Paul with some help from the Zen Buddhist Shin-ichi Hisamatsu (1889–1980).

6. Ibid.

7. Ibid., pp. 121f.

8. Ibid., p. 122.

Response I

—

John B. Cobb, Jr

What is most striking about our four essays is their general congruence in comparison with the wide sweep of contemporary theological opinion. It is hard to generate sharp controversy when we agree on so much. Perhaps the leadership of the Vatican Secretariat has gone so far and done so well that the rest of us have only to follow! And perhaps for that reason our differences are only minor or a matter of emphasis. To pry open these differences so as to develop issues for debate seems questionable. My first inclination is to express agreement and then lapse into silence. Still, since I am committed to write a more extended critique, I will hope that the reader may benefit by seeing how even those who share in a common project for quite similar reasons may yet differ, and how these differences may have practical as well as theoretical dimensions. Discussion of such differences can refine and advance a shared position in a healthy way.

    1. I find in both Knitter and Hellwig a certain disparagement of purely intellectual or doctrinal dialogue. Knitter wants to orient the dialogue on the urgent issues of the day. Hellwig stresses the need for involvement in one another's practice. I do not wish in any way to minimize the types of dialogue they describe. As long as I can take what they have written as expressive of personal preference for particular approaches, I simply affirm both. But I detect in the rhetoric of both a tendency to generalize their personal preferences in such a way as to disparage the preferences of others. I feel that my own approach and experience are belittled by both in somewhat different ways. I feel that I am being told by Knitter that I *should* not have sought to understand central ideas and insights of another tradition in relative isolation from the urgent social and ecological crises that threaten us all. I feel that I am being told by Hellwig that I *cannot* understand what my dialogue partners say because I have not practiced their spiritual disciplines.

    I do not flatly disagree with either point. In response to Knitter I agree that to do *any* thinking today that is not relevant to our global crises is finally unChristian. But it may be that at times we can contribute most by dealing with particular questions that are only indirectly related to those crises. It may be that transforming Christian self-understanding on basic theological issues may do as much or more to heal the world as would explicit discussion with others about these issues. But none of these comments diminishes in any way the importance of *also* engaging in the dialogue for which Knitter calls. As long as Knitter is, as he says, *proposing* one form of dialogue without *opposing* others, I endorse his proposal wholeheartedly.

I am sure that Hellwig is correct in suggesting that since I have not engaged in the practice of my dialogue partners, I do not truly understand them, and I commend those whose extensive practice opens this avenue of understanding. But understanding is a matter of degree, and practice is as much informed by theory as theory is by practice. It is not clear that extensive Zen sitting on the part of Christians insures their understanding of Zen concepts or non-concepts. And it does not seem to be the case that nothing is learned in verbal discussion. Again, I plead only for a further openness to a multiplicity of approaches, all of which are partial.

My concern here is more for what these papers say to our dialogue partners from other religious traditions than for what they say to Christians who would engage in dialogue. There are some Hindus who would feel that Knitter's focus does not express the deepest Hindu insight. Do we preclude listening to them? However convinced we are about our position, is it not better to be open to hearing what a critic has to say?

Similarly, while it may be well for Christians to chide other Christians for not entering into the practice of other religious communities, is it desirable to tell dialogue partners that they can understand what we have to say only at the price of living with us for some time? Perhaps at some point such comments are helpful. But for the most part it seems better to engage in conversation freely and openly, pressing its potentialities as far as possible.

I wonder why it is so important to so many Christians to identify one way as *the* right way to engage in dialogue. Why can we not encourage many types of dialogue? Why can we not respect one another fully in our differences of temperament, of style, and of interest? Is that not the more catholic approach?

2. I particularly rejoice that Swidler does not insist on a pre-established common ground as a basis for dialogue. On the contrary, he recognizes complementarity as an alternative mode in which religious traditions can be related. He properly recognizes that there may also be contradictions, while warning us against too quickly treating differences in that way.

Knitter, on the other hand, first tells us that he has given up the quest for a foundation for dialogue, and then returns to the search for a common basis. The intensity of his drive to unity already appears in the second of his four pivotal elements in dialogue: "The *trust* that such differences are unitive rather than separative" (p. 19). Must we have *this* trust in order to enter dialogue? Can we not engage in dialogue to find out whether our differences are unitive or separative? Is it not enough to trust that our partner speaks with some wisdom, saying something that we need to hear?

Knitter's urge to find commonality as the basis for dialogue expresses itself again when he seeks a "common core" in all religions. The distinction between a common core and a foundation is not entirely clear. But what he in fact comes up with here is quite different from what "common core" has usually meant. He speaks of the "common core" as a shared global context. That there is such a context is a point of agreement between us.

The limitation of this commonality is, however, that the perception and valuation of the global context differs among potential participants in dialogue. These differences could, of course, be the subject of discussion. But that is not what Knitter has in mind. He wants to define the common context and have agreement on that definition as the basis for dialogue about how to respond. This does seem to be a new form of the imperialism that he wants to avoid.

Knitter's quest for a common ground, despite his initial disclaimer, expresses itself again in his call for a soteriocentric basis for the dialogue. I am confident that this works better than the theocentric one he has abandoned. I agree that all religious traditions have some idea of a wrongness of whose correction they speak. If one cannot bring oneself to speak to one's neighbor without predefining some commonality, this one will serve. I continue to wonder why this is necessary and how it advances the dialogue. Knitter does not mean to focus the discussion on how the several traditions have defined the problem in the past but rather on how they are responding to the range of issues he outlines. Can this not be done even among discussants not all of whom define themselves as soteriocentric?

Hellwig is still more explicit in identifying the assumption of commonality as the grounds of openness to dialogue. Dialogue "is based on the conviction that we have a common starting point and a common end in the transcendent ultimate," and that "what is truly ultimate is unified so that all quests for communion with the ultimate are in process of converging" (p. 51). Is this so? If dialogue is limited to the theistic traditions, this assumption may work. But there are many Buddhists who do not understand themselves as seeking communion with the ultimate. Also, it is hard to see in what sense their starting point is the same as that of most Christians. Can we not approach dialogue with an open mind, allowing our partners to define their starting points and their goals and then reflecting together on whether they are the same or different? Hellwig thinks that the many traditions represent "many paths to salvation, many ways of worshipping the same ultimate, transcendent reality, many languages and rituals by which peoples search for communion with the divine and respond to the outreach of the divine in creation" (p. 51). But can we not enter dialogue open to the possibility that what is offered by the partner is a different path to a different goal, a different name of a different aspect of reality, a different language through which something quite different from communion is sought? Does not this possibility add interest to dialogue?

3. Although in point 2 my sharpest disagreement is with Hellwig, I strongly agree with her that it is a serious mistake to identify particular beliefs (or rejection of particular beliefs) as the prerequisite for Christians to enter into dialogue with others. With regard to rejecting traditional doctrines as a precondition of dialogue, Hellwig writes: "The disadvantage is that it is very difficult to find a convincing justification for claiming authority to stand above the tradition and judge it . . . This kind of approach usually necessitates a sharp break . . . As an approach to dialogue this is very indirect, because it begins with an argument that takes a long time to soften into amicable conversation within the tradition before there can be conversation with those outside the tradition" (p. 52). Both Knitter and Swidler seem to fall into this trap.

When Swidler argues that only those who have a de-absolutized view of truth *want* to engage in dialogue, he is partly correct, but not wholly so. Certainly there are those who see no point in listening to others, assuming in advance that insofar as the others say anything different from what they themselves already believe, the others must be in error. But the issue is not whether one holds some truth as absolute but whether one supposes oneself to be in possession of all truth worth having. Many of those who think that they have *some* absolute truth still acknowledge that more is still to be learned. These are not closed to learning. If the absolute truth tells them that they can only learn through narrowly circumscribed channels, then again they may not be interested in most potential dialogue partners. But that is a special case not to be generalized to all who hold some truths absolutely. One can, for example, believe the Chalcedonian creed in a quite absolutist sense and still want to learn more about God, about Jesus Christ, about humanity in general, about the natural world, or about oneself. A wide field of dialogue is open.

I may be disputing Knitter's view more sharply than Swidler's here. In describing the conditions of dialogue Knitter writes: "First of all, religious believers cannot approach the table of dialogue with claims (on or below the table!) of having 'the final word,' or the 'definitive revelation,' or the 'absolute truth,' or the 'absolute savior'" (p. 31). Clearly this restricts the possibility of fruitful dialogue to one rather small segment of the Christian community – often to those who have already been deeply affected by dialogue. Yet precisely the other, more mainstream, part of the community may be most in need of dialogue. Is it really true that its members "cannot" approach the table of dialogue without first passing through a theological conversion? I hope – and believe – that Knitter is mistaken.

I am particularly troubled that he makes explicit his demand on the representatives of other traditions as well: "It would seem, therefore, that the revision of traditional understandings of 'the uniqueness of Christ and

Christianity' (together with similar understandings of the Qur'an or of Krishna or of Buddha) is a condition for the possibility of fruitful dialogue" (p. 32). What does this mean? Does it mean that we are not interested in talking with Muslims who take seriously the "uniqueness of the Qu'ran?" Then where can we find Muslim conversation partners? Have we not predecided that we are not interested in dialogue with the real Muslim community when we lay down such conditions? What have we gained by that? I for one am not willing to restrict my own dialogue so narrowly.

Of course, my disagreement with Knitter here is much subtler than these formulations suggest. Knitter is writing of conditions for "fruitful" dialogue. I agree that the most enjoyable and personally rewarding dialogues take place among people who enter dialogue genuinely willing to learn from one another and willing to revise their own beliefs in light of what they learn, and especially when this willingness extends over large areas of faith. But the difference remains. What Knitter calls for as conditions of fruitful dialogue I see as a possible outcome of dialogue. Furthermore, some of Knitter's language suggests an outcome I would deplore rather than celebrate. In particular I affirm and celebrate the uniqueness of Christ, of Christianity, of the Qu'ran, of Krishna, and of Buddha. To surrender any of these in their uniqueness either as a condition or as an outcome of dialogue seems to me a loss to be keenly regretted.

Again, my main point is not that Swidler and Knitter are misrepresenting the conditions of an ideal dialogue, although there are some formulations I would need to qualify considerably. My main point is that when quite traditional Christians are interested in dialogue, it is not for us to discourage them by announcing that they *cannot* dialogue. Indeed, Jews, Muslims, and others are often at least as interested in conversation with conservatives as with progressives. They want to hear from conservative Christians how they think about a wide range of matters. And they want conservative Christians to hear how they think as well.

If we reverse the picture, this should be quite understandable. In our desire to understand Jews, Muslims, and others, we realize that our dialogue partners are often the most liberal members of those communities, but we are not necessarily pleased with that. We want also to understand and learn from the most traditional members of these communities.

Furthermore, important dialogue is not limited to those who pre-decide that the partner's faith has rough parity with their own. A Christian convinced of the superiority of Christianity can profit from dialogue with a Hindu equally convinced of the superiority of Hinduism. It may be that experience with one another will moderate their respective claims, but that is a possible result of dialogue, not a precondition.

Indeed, I find too much concern in both Swidler and Knitter with the conditions of dialogue. Much of what is said, of course, describes what they consider to be the ideal dialogue, and both have every right to share their dreams. But these ideal dialogues will involve only a small percentage of the members of any religious community. In most cases these will be those with the greatest knowledge of other traditions. Is it not better to encourage whatever interest there may be in dialogue across the whole spectrum of theological views? We can then hope that the actual experience of dialogue will lead to greater conformity with what we severally consider the ideal conditions of dialogue. But it is not for us to predetermine the outcome.

Let me hasten to say that I do not deny that there are conditions for dialogue, but I find them to be very minimal. Both parties must be prepared to listen respectfully to one another and to share honestly. Swidler and Knitter offer much excellent advice beyond this, but the occurrence of dialogue is not dependent on any further conditions.

Perhaps I can summarize all my concerns with the essays of my colleagues in a single analogy. Let us think of what Knitter calls the table of dialogue as a table of communion. Among Protestants there are two different attitudes toward admittance to this table. One is to "fence" the table, that is, to specify the condition on which people may come. The purpose is to insure that only those who are worthy to commune will do so. The other attitude is to encourage all who will to come. This is called "open" communion. In this view none are worthy, but all can become more nearly worthy through communion itself.

In varying ways and degrees I see all three of my colleagues as "fencing" the table. They are all concerned with worthiness for dialogue. I, on the other hand, belong to a Protestant tradition that emphasizes "open" communion. Let whosoever will join the conversation!

Response I

—

Paul F. Knitter

Having read and pondered the statements on dialogue by John Cobb, Monika Hellwig, and Len Swidler, I have, as expected, an immediate and heartening sense of solidarity. Clearly we are on the same team, sharing the same vision, working at the same task. We are in agreement on the basics: on recognizing the *necessity* of interreligious dialogue, on locating its *purpose* in an understanding and cooperation that will transform the religions *and* the world, and on trying to remove the *obstacles* to dialogue inherent in the absolute or exclusive content of traditional Christian claims. But while we are on the same team trying to win the same game, there are evident differences in the way we understand the game-plan. To me, it seems that most of those differences hover around "how-to" issues: how to go about dialogue fruit-fully and how to deal effectively with Christians' traditional claims of finality and superiority.

To make our own dialogue profitable, I will focus on our differences. In trying to identify and then resolve our disagreements, we can learn from each other and clarify and strengthen our game-plan. Our differences, in Swidler's terminology, are much more complementary than contradictory.

How to do it?

I would first like to point out what I think is the *presupposition* or *precondition* for dialogue that all three of my colleagues either explicitly or implicitly affirm in the goals they set up for interreligious encounter. For all of them, religious believers engage one another in order to foster understanding (at least), agreement (at best), and cooperation (at last). In order to propose, and especially to pursue, these goals, my colleagues implicitly recognize that there must be something that the religions have *in common*, some shared context or basis because of which religious believers can reach across the chasm of their differences to understand and embrace and work with each other. All three of my colleagues, it seems to me, are presupposing some kind of commonality among the religions – a commonality that transcends doctrinal expression or ritual-ethical practice.

Monika Hellwig affirms such commonality most clearly – and perhaps, therefore, most dangerously – when she expresses "the conviction that we have a *common starting point* in human experience and a *common end* in the transcendent ultimate" (p. 51, emphasis mine). She is well aware that such a position is "based on an act of faith" – a faith which affirms that "what is truly ultimate" is so "unified . . . that all quests for communion with the ultimate are in process of converging" (ibid.). Evidently Hellwig believes that such an act of faith can be found in all religious traditions; otherwise she could not propose it as a "common starting point." Here she will have to face the same critics whom I have encountered in making similar proposals – critics who warn that the notion of the "Ultimate" in other traditions may be understood quite differently than in Christianity, perhaps as grounding not ever greater "convergence" or unity but, rather, ever more diversity and pluralism. Is Hellwig's starting point "common" or might it be "imposed"?

Leonard Swidler is more reserved about affirming common ground or starting points. Still, in his many publications on interreligious dialogue, in his recent calls for a "universal theology of religions" and for a common religious "esperanto" among religions,[1] and in his contribution to this discussion, it is evident that for Swidler, as for Arnold Toynbee, if the distinct melodies of each religion of the world could be played together, they would make for much more harmony than cacophony.[2] When he distinguishes religious differences as either "complementary, analogous, or contradictory," he recognizes that contradictions exist and have to be faced, but he suggests that they are "relatively rare" (pp. 68f.). For Swidler, there seems to be something that makes the differences between religious traditions much more unifying than estranging.

Of the four of us, John Cobb is perhaps the most wary in talking about religious commonalities. I owe him much for increasing my own wariness about affirming common ground or goals among religions.[3] On the one hand, he becomes nervous on hearing fellow Christians talk about "one reality" or one truth within all religions. The "one" reality all too easily, all too unconsciously, becomes "my" reality. So he begins his contribution to this volume by affirming that dialogue must always include confrontation – the honest recognition of differences, differences that can speak to each other precisely because they are different. Cobb refuses to gloss over differences or hastily to distill some common substance out of them.

On the other hand, Cobb is also aware that the differences can be so stark that they lead to incompatibility or incommensurability. At this point, his response is interesting. Without explaining why, Cobb tells us that we must *resist* incompatibility and affirm unity: ". . . it is a serious mistake to accept incompatibility as final in any given instance without the most intensive efforts to find another solution." These intensive efforts are based on what Cobb calls the "inner impulse of dialogue," which is "to proceed to that point at which the central intentions and convictions of both partners can be affirmed without contradictions." He believes (or trusts? or presupposes?) that a "point" exists where "the deepest insights of each are compatible with one another" (p. 4). At such a point, we do not necessarily have two different expressions of the same truth; rather, we have truth "cohering" in two different positions; the two positions are "compatible without being identical" (p. 6).

What enables him to presuppose and search for this underlying compatibility among the deepest insights of religions? Here Cobb becomes difficult to pin down. In trying to point to such compatibility between the utterly different notions of Zen Emptiness and the Christian God, he writes: "Is it not conceivable that in the *full complexity of reality*, so far exceeding all that we can know or think, 'Emptying' identifies one truly important aspect, and 'God' another? I think so" (p. 6, emphasis mine). This "full complexity of reality" would seem to be the common, shared reality that holds such differing religious experiences together and enables them to speak to and influence each other. Cobb's trust that this "reality" can do this is no doubt influenced by his Christian belief that "reality" includes a "God" who, as Cobb reminds us, calls us to the radical risk of dialogue; and in that dialogue, Cobb insists further, we are not really trusting this God if we refuse to let the heat of dialogue touch even beliefs considered to be absolute or non-negotiable. For Cobb, therefore, there is a Reality that enables religious believers committed to dialogue to hope that incompatibility will, for the most part, give way to compatibility. One would like to hear more from Cobb as to how this "Reality" works, or how one might tune into it in order to promote the compatibility and mutual transformation of religions.

This is the question I would like to explore with my colleagues: granting that we all recognize that the pursuit of interreligious dialogue is grounded in something that makes the enterprise possible and worthwhile, how can we tune ourselves to that "something" so as to be able to understand and transform each other? How do we go about dialogue? How do we *act* on the presupposition that there is something that makes it possible and valuable? Let me attempt to state how I think each of my colleagues tries to answer these questions and then comment on what appear to be the strengths and weaknesses of their answers. I am hoping that through this exchange a better game-plan will result.

For Swidler, interreligious dialogue is still primarily an encounter of minds and ideas and beliefs – an intellectual pursuit which, however, is not to remain only intellectual. But that is where we start. He defines the purpose of dialogue as "learning more truth about the subject from the other" (p. 57) and holds that "communication in ideas and words" is "indeed the primary meaning of dialogue" (p. 56). True, he immediately adds that if this communication does not lead to "action and spirituality" it is "sterile." But the implication is that action or spiritual exchange will be the outcome of the primary exchange in "ideas and words." In fact, when Swidler urges a "soteriocentric dialogue" in which the "action" we strive for is understood as "salvation," he defines salvation in a rather intellectual fashion – as "the search for ultimate meaning in life" (rather than as the transformation of life, as liberation theologians would). Also, in urging religious people to take up "joint action" he cautions that they can do so only after the action "has been found congruent with each tradition's principles and warranted in the concrete circumstances" (p. 67). Again, action follows theoretical discussion.

Swidler's more intellectual-theoretical understanding of dialogue is also the reason why it is so important for him that before religious partners sit down at the table of dialogue, they first clear their religious decks of any "absolutist" trump cards. He wants intellectual clarity and honesty about such absolutist impediments before the game can begin. Truth has to be deabsolutized in everyone's minds before we can start thinking. Although I am in hearty agreement with Swidler about the roadblocks that absolute claims set up for dialogue, I am not so sure that the first step in getting the encounter moving is to remove them. In fact, I think the first steps are to be made elsewhere. And that is my fundamental question for Swidler.

In line with my opening statement and with what I think is one of the central insights of the reformation of Christianity contained in liberation theology, I would urge that dialogue, like theology, is a second step. Our first step should be some form of shared liberative praxis; we begin by hearing the cry of the oppressed people or the oppressed earth and by responding together. The ultimate purpose of dialogue, therefore, is not *learning* more truth but *doing* more truth. The "primary meaning of dialogue" is not "communication in ideas and words" but the transformation of our world. Perhaps the differences between Swidler and me derive from the way we perceive our present world. When he holds that "joint action" is possible only if it is congruent with the religions' principles and warranted by the context, I would suggest that it *is* congruent with the principles of all religions to respond to suffering and injustice and nuclear threat and that the "concrete circumstances" of our presently threatened globe *do demand* such "joint action" on the part of all religions. If religions do not so respond, they can be accused of theological infidelity to their tradition and of immoral insensitivity to the victims of the earth. (I say this, of course, as a Christian; I hope there will be believers from other traditions who will say the same.)

Swidler indirectly recognizes the possibility and efficacy of such a primacy of praxis for dialogue. Together with Hans Küng, he notes that religious believers, together with humanity in general, are "painfully slowly creeping toward a consensus on what is involved in an authentically full human life. The 1948 United Nations Declaration of Human Rights was an important step in that direction" (p. 70).[4] On the basis of such a growing consensus –

which can never be absolutized and which must be constantly refined through dialogue – adherents of different traditions can make a common commitment to overcoming what they have defined as "hostile to human life." When they do this and when they act together against all that threatens life, the door is open to deeper and more effective "communication in words and ideas."

Swidler himself illustrates this with his example of dialogue in the concentration camps. The dialogue began not with discussions of the Jewish and Christian notions of the Messiah or of the Trinity, but with their shared suffering and with the effort, limited though it was, to do something about that suffering. In their shared struggle against the evil of the Third Reich, they discovered what it was they had in common; they were able to hear and understand each other as never before. This is an example of a "soteriocentric dialogue" and its possibilities.

Hellwig is even more explicit and firm than Swidler in giving priority to the goals of dialogue and in subordinating praxis to theory in procedure. As the first two goals of dialogue she lists: "to gain a friendly understanding of others" and "to round out one's appreciation of one's own faith tradition." Only after realizing these two gains can we move to the third and set about establishing a "community of life and action among persons of various traditions" (p. 47). If I understand her correctly, Hellwig would have serious reservations about my appeal for a soteriocentric primacy of praxis, for she adamantly warns that the third goal of common action

> ... cannot be the immediate goal but can *only grow out of the other two*. A common ground for action, for instance in matters of social justice or peace or routine administration of affairs in a larger society, can really *only* be established when there has been a growing appreciation for the values and worldview of the other tradition. It is tempting but *counter-productive to move swiftly to the third goal*, establishing only a very superficial and flimsy common basis for action. . . . A sharing of ideals and values is the best way of finding what is really in common between two traditions (p. 48, emphasis mine).

Like Swidler, Hellwig holds up a sharing of ideals and values as the goal of dialogue; but she differs from Swidler in the way she hopes to achieve this sharing. Her entrée into dialogue is not primarily *intellectual*, through an exchange of words and ideas (Swidler); nor is it *ethical*, through shared liberative praxis (Knitter); rather, it is *mystical-ritual*, through the sharing of ritual, life, and story. Her proposal is essentially that of John Dunne's method of "passing over" to the experience of another religion by entering, via imagination, into the stories, the symbols, the ritual of the other religion and then "passing back" to test out the gained insights within one's own tradition. For Hellwig, through such "intensive exercises of imagination" we find that the "elements of [our own] experience are rearranged in different configurations" (p. 49). So for her, the "common starting point" by which religious persons can touch and understand that which they have in common is a personal, experiential exploration of each other's symbols and stories. Such a mystical-ritual starting point is clearly preferred to opening the dialogue with efforts to understand the "codes of life and behavior that traditions have constructed for themselves," since "codes tend to establish boundaries rather than highlight the center" (p. 49f.).

Knowing and sharing Hellwig's own commitment to both the method and content of liberation theology, I am hoping that I can enlist her help in trying to forge, from a Christian perspective, greater bonds between interreligious dialogue and liberation theology. In posing the following questions, I am asking whether she can aid me in developing what I have called a liberation-centered encounter among religions. Both of us are in basic agreement that "the fundamental or primary path to mutual understanding" between religions is *not* "the exchange of theologies" (p. 50) – that is, not an academic or intellectual exchange. One grasps truth, one understands the value of another person or culture or religion by somehow *living* that truth, by feeling it, by entering into it. For Hellwig, religious persons can do this by entering into each other's rituals and stories. My question for her is this: Is this the only way? Is this a sufficient way? Cannot we experience the possible truth of another religion by entering into the way that truth is lived out in its ethical applications? In fact, is not this passing over to another religion's ethical response to suffering and injustice a necessary condition for fully grasping what its rituals and myths really contain?

Within a Christian context, I think Hellwig would respond positively to these questions. In fact, she has written eloquently and challengingly that we cannot really know and experience what the eucharist means if we limit ourselves to celebrating it within the walls of a church; the eucharist must be lived out in a commitment to sharing bread with the hungry.[5] Only then have we experienced eucharist. Nor can we grasp the content of the gospel stories and New Testament myths simply by retelling them and feeling their power to stir our imagination toward undreamed-of possibilities; we have to live the stories and test those possibilities in our own life's story; we have to apply the stories to our own world of suffering and sin. If this is so of Christian ritual and story, would it not also apply to our efforts to grasp the rituals and stories of other traditions? In order to understand a Muslim ritual, I must also grasp how that ritual influences the way Muslims deal with their concrete life situation, with suffering and hunger. In order to pass over to the Buddhist story of Gautama, I must see how that story is being lived out in confronting poverty, e.g., in Sri Lanka.

In other words, our starting point is not only mystical-ritual, it is also praxic. The three must go together (and therefore I can be faulted for not sufficiently recognizing the role of mystical prayer and ritual in my emphasis on liberative action). I think Hellwig has said much the same thing in an excellent review article she wrote on liberation theology some years ago; in quoting a passage from it, I would like to substitute terms from our present discussion: "The life of prayer and faith [read: the life of ritual and story] are not seen as side by side with social concerns [read: liberative praxis] but as coincident with them [it]. Theology [read: dialogue] is not found alongside the concern with the causes of suffering but arises out of that concern."[6]

I think I am only applying to our question of interreligious dialogue an "epistemological and hermeneutic principle" which Hellwig herself would endorse: "namely, that truth is in action."[7] If truth is not really grasped only in theory, but always through a blending of theory and praxis, then I do not understand how she can hold that her first two goals of "understanding" and "appreciation" can be achieved without a concomitant "community of life and action." Unless I am misunderstanding her, I would have to disagree that "codes tend to establish boundaries rather than highlight the center" (p. 50). As I mentioned in my opening essay, the experience of "base human communities" in Asia indicates that it is in passing over to the way Buddhist peasants are applying the Four Noble Truths to their socio-political problems that Christians are "passing over" to the center of Buddhist experience. We can, I think, "pass over" not only to ritual and story but also to code and practice; our imagination can be stirred by action as well as by contemplation.

John Cobb's carefully crafted suggestions concerning the "how to" of dialogue – how we might search for deeper compatibilities underlying foreboding differences – are both realistic and insightful. Recognizing that each religion holds up something that is "supremely important" and that these supremely important claims will generally differ according to the religions' different contexts and fundamental questions, Cobb offers us the simple suggestion that what is supremely important in someone else's religion need not threaten what is supremely important in ours. In fact, Cobb seems happy to point out that when the contexts of two religions are markedly different – e.g. between Hinduism and Christianity – there will most likely be no clash of supremely important claims at all (p. 10).

Cobb realistically recognizes that most believers feel their revelations or enlightenment to be supremely important not only for themselves but for everyone else; he suggests, cautiously, that we all adopt a "provisional bracketing of judgment" on such convictions. This will enable us to "adopt an attitude of openness to the theoretical possibility that what Hindus have learned and experienced is of comparable interest and importance" (p. 11). In other words, Cobb is urging his fellow Christians and all believers to open themselves to the possibility that there may be *multiple* supremely important revelations – or in terms that Cobb has used elsewhere, multiple absolutes. This is Cobb's way of carrying out Swidler's admonition that we have to lay down our absolute cards if we are going to take up the game of dialogue.

What Cobb is suggesting here is, if I may put it this way, of "supreme importance" for the success of interreligious dialogue. The issues and questions I now raise are intended to facilitate his project and, perhaps, push it forward. First of all, a peripheral, though important, comment: in rejoicing over the fact that our "supremely important" claims are so different as not to threaten each other, Cobb is affirming and embracing the reality of pluralism. Reality abounds in a profligate manyness – a manyness that can never be neatly or coherently related. While I agree with Cobb about such ontological pluralism, I would also want to point out the danger of embracing it too readily. There is a real danger among us bourgeois liberals of overindulging in plurality and diversity and so blinding ourselves to the conflict, injustice, or oppression that all too often lurks below the surface of such diversity. Within the plurality of cultures and religions, there is not only the exuberance of truth but also the din of conflict and ideological abuse. To recognize differing viewpoints, therefore, will often mean to have to choose between them. There are limits to pluralism and to tolerance. There is, in other words, a danger of us liberals playing our pluralistic fiddles while Rome and the world burn.

But I know that given the way liberation theology has affected John Cobb's theological identity, he is well aware of such dangers. He admits that his suggestion that we should "bracket" the absoluteness of our truth-claims does not solve the problem of what to do when there *is* a clash of such claims. Nor does it resolve the question of whether, in our contemporary, threatened world, some claims are universally more "important" than others. These are the questions I would raise for Cobb: how might we deal with such situations of conflict? How might we make judgments as to when and how much my claims need to be "transformed" or corrected by those of another tradition? More fundamentally, I would ask Cobb to provide more help in determining how we can understand other beliefs and practices that are so utterly different from our own. Here is where I think my suggestions for a "soteriocentric" or liberation-centered approach to dialogue might "cohere" with and complement Cobb's method of dialogue.

I would base my hopes for this coherence on what Cobb said about the role of one's understanding of "salvation" in dialogue. He admits that for those who view salvation in an "objectivist" and other-worldly fashion, there will be little interest in dialogue; to such people, Cobb confesses, "I have little to say" (p. 13). The notion of salvation, however, that will make for effective dialogue, recognizes salvation "as something we participate in *here and now* rather than, or in addition to, life beyond." For such people, salvation will "identify what is most precious and supremely valuable *in human life here and now* or that for which *they most deeply hope*" (p. 13, emphasis mine). Cobb here proposes, indirectly, that effective dialogue will prosper among religious persons who affirm that salvation must take place in this world. He seems to be suggesting that the affirmation of this-worldly salvation is a "precondition" for dialogue; he evidently feels that followers within all religions can accept such a precondition (which does not mean that *all* religious believers *will* accept it).

I would like to push Cobb's proposal a step further. Granting the threatened, suffering, explosive state of our contemporary world (and we have no choice, it seems, but to "grant" it!), could not and would not religious believers from all the traditions recognize among themselves as they sit down for dialogue that whatever else "salvation" in this world means, it must address the need for human, ecological, and nuclear liberation? Admitting, as Cobb reminds us, that each religion will perceive such need and such liberation differently, they would still be able to begin their dialogue in agreement that such need must be confronted and that the religions of the world have something to contribute to that confrontation.

This salvation- or liberation-centered starting point would give the religious conversation a basis for both recognizing the apparent differences between the many models of salvation *and* for searching for what Cobb presumes is the compatibility between the deepest insights within these models. It is on the basis of concern for liberation-*soteria* that we can realize how two traditions can be "compatible without being identical" (p. 6). A soteriocentric approach would foster Cobb's hopes for dialogue; it would enable religions to *understand* each other despite their bewildering differences. But such an approach would also enable the religions to *judge* each other, and so avoid what Cobb calls "the corrosive acids of relativism" (p. 4). The criteria for such judgments would be whether or how much a particular doctrine or practice really does promote the welfare of humanity and the world. Admittedly, there are no absolute criteria here; in fact, they would have to be worked out and progressively agreed upon within the dialogue. But if, as Swidler and Küng assure us, there is a growing consensus among nations and religions as to what is necessary for a "full humanity," then there is growing hope that the religions can share criteria for evaluating each other.

A shared commitment to *soteria* or liberation, therefore, can help maintain the delicate tensions involved in trying to follow Swidler's admonition to abandon all absolutes without falling into relativism. No notion of "salvation" or "human fulfillment" can ever be absolute or final; and yet in our shared "absolute" commitments to promoting salvation we can discover tenuous, ever-developing criteria for making cautious judgments as to what is true or false, i.e. what does or does not promote liberation.

What to do about the uniqueness of Jesus?

Although we are all agreed that traditional models for understanding the uniqueness of Christ and Christianity have formed roadblocks to a genuine encounter with other traditions, I am not sure that we would all agree how those roadblocks are to be removed. Again, my questions are raised in order to build inter-Christian agreement which will foster interreligious dialogue.

I have little doubt about Swidler's position on how we are to understand and reform traditional claims concerning the uniqueness of Jesus Christ. With his reminder that all the New Testament language about Jesus is literary metaphor, he frees us to take this language seriously but not literally or absolutely (p. 17). And with the theological ontology that he derives from Katsumi Takizawa and Seichi Yagi (which, I think, is in essential agreement with and more coherent than Karl Rahner's transcendental christology), Swidler pushes his case further by showing that the "primary contact" between God and the self of Jesus is common to all persons, while Jesus' "secondary contact" (the full realization of the primary contact) might well have been – or could still be – realized by others. Jesus is unique, therefore, without being exclusively unique. Although I would want to remind Swidler that even though we may not want to take New Testament language about Jesus literally, the early Christians did, and although I would want to explore more than he does the ontological content of New Testament literary metaphors about Jesus, I am in basic agreement with him. On the issue of de-absolutizing Jesus (which does not mean diluting his importance and salvific power), Swidler is the boldest and most demanding among us.

John Cobb resonates with Swidler's approach to the New Testament witness, for like Swidler he recognizes that the titles given to Jesus were "existential" and "doxological" before they were used to evaluate him above all other religious figures (p. 12). And when Cobb contemplates the way "the affirmations of metaphysical uniqueness of Jesus grew out of doxological statements," he implies that such growth may not have been entirely proper – that perhaps the metaphysics far outstripped the doxology. Cobb evidently prefers the personalism of doxology to the absoluteness of metaphysics; perhaps this is why he could suggest that Christians "bracket" their beliefs that theirs is the only "supremely important" revelation for all peoples and open themselves to the possibility that other religions may also have "supremely important" messages for all humankind. When Cobb concludes that "in this sense they [believers involved in dialogue] give up their exclusive claims," he is taking what has been called "the pluralist turn" in Christian theology of religions. He is recognizing that traditional claims about Jesus' finality and superiority are not essential to Christian belief and practice.

Or is he? Toward the end of this chapter, he becomes somewhat slippery on this point. Although he earlier urged Christians to bracket their claims that their revelation is "more" supremely important than others, he later states "that [it] is a legitimate starting point for dialogue" for Christians to hold that in Jesus Christ they have "the truth of the everlasting and universal Word with *unique fullness*" (pp. 17–18, emphasis mine). My problem is not with the word "unique" but with "fullness." I am not sure what he means, for he adds that the "unique fullness in Jesus" can not only be "reinforced" by the truth found in other traditions, it can also be "supplemented" (p. 18). Supposing that he consciously chose the word "supplement" over "complement," I would ask Cobb how something can be "full" if it is "supplemented" or added to? Would it not be more coherent with what he said about "bracketing" claims of finality and with the requirements of the dialogical process to drop all talk of "fullness." From what we can tell of our experience of God and of our knowledge of history, *no one has the full truth*. Do we have to put such a statement in "brackets" in order to say it? Can we not just say it forthrightly, and really mean it?

In our shared concerns to reinterpret traditional views of the uniqueness of Christ, I feel I have more in common with Swidler and Cobb than with Hellwig; therefore I have more to learn from her than from the others. On this point, Hellwig is the most pastorally sensitive and theologically cautious. I cannot but applaud the pastoral concerns in her reminder that theologians cannot stand before the Christian community and simply announce that all past claims about the uniqueness or absoluteness of Christ are wrong. Such a tack would be disruptive of the community; more practically, it would not be "received" – people would not listen. Hellwig has pointed this out to me in the past, and I have tried to listen and learn. In her book *Jesus the Compassion of God*, she writes: ". . . to claim only that Jesus offers a way of salvation to us which is one among many is to fall short of fidelity to the classic statements about Jesus in the Bible and the tradition."[8] And in a personal letter some years ago, she explained:

I theologize decidedly from inside the tradition, and am unwilling to set out any theory which I think the Catholic community of believers (the community we actually have, with its actual hierarchic structure) cannot possibly accept as consonant with its faith . . . we come to the anchor of Christian faith when we speak of the uniqueness of Jesus Christ. I am prepared to suggest different ways of formulating what that uniqueness consists of, and I am prepared to present our conviction of the centrality of Jesus Christ in history as a friendly wager with outsiders who do not see history and salvation in that perspective. If I were [however] to say that Christians do not really, ultimately, see Jesus Christ as central or unique, this would not, I think, be true in fact.

Baum makes a similar point:

It seems to me that the churches become agents of political and cultural change only if their prophets, their daring thinkers, their innovators, speak from the center of the tradition. Their reinterpretation must verify itself in the religious experiences of the people. The people must recognize in the new position the religion they have inherited. [Therefore] While I fully recognize the need for dialogue . . . and cooperation between Christians and members of other religions, I am not prepared to give up the Christo-centric perspective we have inherited.[9]

Given the venerable Christian tradition that the teachings of both bishops and theologians must be "received" by the community of faithful before they are finally validated, Hellwig's and Baum's admonitions go to the heart of contemporary efforts to reinterpret the meaning of Christ within a world of many religions.

So Hellwig proposes what she feels is a more pastorally attuned procedure. She first rules out two moves as pastorally unacceptable and ineffective: either flat-out to deny the truth of absolute claims about Jesus (as it might appear people like Swidler and I do) or to argue that in the sweep of historical development such claims may have been meaningful at one time but are no longer necessary today. Rather, she suggests that theologians show – through exegetical, hermeneutic and contextual analysis – that traditional texts which have long grounded Christian exclusivism have actually been misunderstood. Her example of how the proclamation opening the so-called Athanasian Creed about no salvation outside the Catholic faith has been misperceived and abused is insightful and sobering. There are two reasons, however, why I suspect that her pastoral plan may not do its intended job.

First, I wonder just how pastorally convincing and reassuring such exegetical, hermeneutic, and contextual analyses will be for the common faithful. Patterns of hearing and understanding texts such as "one and only Son of God" or "Those who are not baptized will be condemned" (Mark 16:16) have entrenched themselves in the sensitivities of the Christian community over the centuries. I fear that theologians who come along and announce, on the basis of their historical studies, that such texts have for the most part been misunderstood will not score high on the trust scale of ordinary Christians. "They're at it again," might be a general response, "undermining our traditional beliefs with high-class scholarship."

Perhaps I am too paranoid about how to approach my community of faith. So let's say that Hellwig's suggestions *can* work. I would still have a second reservation: do they go far enough? At least from her example from the Athanasian Creed, it seems that while she has clearly cleansed the text of its exclusivistic narrowness, it still retains an inclusivistic "claim of superiority." And as Hellwig herself recognizes, ". . . this in itself is not a position most conducive to open dialogue" (p. 54). It is not clear to me, in her opening statement in this volume as well as in other writings, how she has moved beyond inclusivism to a position that is both more conducive to dialogue and pastorally sensitive to the Christian community.

Therefore I am eager to hear from her whether she thinks that a liberation-centered approach to other traditions might be of help for making such a move. I strongly suspect – based on my own limited pastoral experience – that the Christian people can readily understand *and* receive a pastoral approach that measures fidelity to the New Testament witness not mainly in the community's insistence that Jesus is "numero uno" but in its commitment to living and working for the kingdom of God. Such a soteriocentric pastoral approach would encourage Christians to understand the heart of their Christian identity not in an orthodox proclamation that salvation is only or finally to be found in Jesus but in an orthopraxic fidelity to trying to realize that salvation in a world that is threatened by economic, ecological, and nuclear oppression. This is not just high-level theological theorizing; it is a message that can be translated to the level of the classroom and the adult-education course. As the last judgment scene in Matthew implies, our Christian identity and our eternal salvation will be decided not by how faithfully we proclaimed Jesus as the one and only savior but by how faithfully we fed the hungry, clothed the naked, and visited those in prison (Matt. 25:31–46). The more the Christian community can become liberation-centered, the lower will be its anxiety level about exploring the question of "other saviors" (in Christian terms) who, with Jesus, may be necessary for promoting "the fullness of humanity."

All this is not to say that such a soteriocentric pastoral program will be easily implemented. There will be resistance, sometimes bitter and biting – as the US bishops have clearly experienced in the reaction of a large segment of the Catholic community to their pastoral letters on war and peace and on the economy. As Hellwig herself admits, those Christians engaged in interreligious dialogue all too often find themselves on the fringes of their communities. She suggests that this is part of the job description of dialogue. I agree and would therefore urge her and Baum not to be overly concerned about how they will be "received" by the community, for pastors must also be prophets, and theologians must suggest visions that will not only enlighten but disturb the community of believers. Before the Christian community can recognize its faith experience in understandings of Christ that no longer insist on his finality or superiority, the community may have to go through some agonizing and confusing exploration. I suggest that a liberation-centered approach to the question of Jesus' uniqueness can guide that exploration and lessen its agony.

Notes

1. See the volume he edited, *Toward a Universal Theology of Religion*, Maryknoll: Orbis 1987, and his contribution to it, "Interreligious and Interideological Dialogue: The Matrix for All Systematic Reflection Today," pp. 5–50.

2. Arnold Toynbee, *A Study of History*, Vol. 7, London and New York: Oxford University Press 1954, p. 428.

3. See Cobb's "Response" in the discussion about my book *No Other Name?*, *Journal of Ecumenical Studies* 24, 1987, 22–3.

4. See Hans Küng's "What Is True Religion? Toward an Ecumenical Criteriology," in *Toward a Universal Theology of Religion*, pp. 231–50, at 239–43.

5. Monika Hellwig, *The Eucharist and the Hunger of the World*, New York: Paulist Press 1976.

6. Monika Hellwig, "Liberation Theology: An Emerging School," *Scottish Journal of Theology*, Vol. 30, pp. 137–51, at 143.

7. Ibid., p. 145.

8. Wilmington: Michael Glazier 1983, p. 133.

9. Gregory Baum, "The Grand Vision: It Needs Social Action," in *Thomas Berry and the New Cosmology*, Mystic, CT: Twenty-Third Publications 1987, p. 55.

Response I

—

Monika K. Hellwig

The first reaction to reading our earlier essays is of course the realization that this is a conversation among partners who largely think alike. It might be more productive to carry on this kind of exchange with a deeply committed member of the Missouri Lutheran Synod and a representative of the Congregation for the Doctrine of the Faith. What we lose in breadth we may gain in more detailed and persistent pursuit of what is meant and hoped.

A second reaction on my part to the first round of essays is the sense that we should not try to determine too many conditions for dialogue, or even for fruitful dialogue. I tend to read the conditions, goals, means, etc. specified in our papers, and in particular in Swidler's paper, not at all as preliminary or absolute requirements, but rather as encouragement and exhortation by a particular author, from that author's experience and point of view. As we have been invited to contribute essays on these topics, I take it that no one is trying to rule out other approaches or campaigning for some one way of doing things. My understanding is that each is quite simply giving a personal testimony of the desirable from experience. In this spirit I am happy to consider each of the approaches with the particular insights it offers, but I am strongly inclined to remain with my own approach inasmuch as it is drawn from my experience and inasmuch as it rests on a deeply reflected appropriation of the Christian faith. That appropriation is more likely at this late stage of my life to be challenged by actual intimate encounters with other faiths than by a dialogue about dialogue, no matter how penetrating.

Nevertheless, there are some points in each of the other three papers which I find informative and enlightening. I am, for instance, very interested in Knitter's suggestion of the soteriocentric pattern for dialogue. I take him to mean that whatever other differences we may have, we do have in common

Knitter

nuclear capacity for destruction, do confront us all with massive common problems. There is no doubt about what Knitter calls the imperative and the opportunity. Moreover, it is clear that such an approach has a built-in reality principle, in that it should issue in action. There remains, of course, the large question whether these worldly problems will be seen from all religious viewpoints as appropriate matter for religious attention and reflection, or might be regarded by some as irrelevant to the religious quest of life. The very least that must be said for Knitter's suggestion is that it should be tried as widely and as frequently and thoroughly as possible.

A point that I find insightful and helpful in Cobb's paper is the initial juxtaposition of confrontation and dialogue with the observation that confrontation also has its role in human relations and can be constructive. This probably needs to be said in our own times and culture more frequently than is the case. Likewise the emphasis that dialogue carries risk is well taken; there is risk not only of having to abandon cherished positions for a greater access to truth, but of being misled by enthusiasm or particularly persuasive rhetoric into blind alleys of confusion.

In the attempt to set out the Christian assumptions for dialogue with others I find Cobb less clear. That may be in part because he seems to draw general principles for dialogue from the particular encounter with Zen Buddhists. Is there really any difference between the assertion "that there is a reality distinct from human opinions about it, and that in one way or another human beings are involved with that reality" (p. 5), and the positions, rather ambiguously described, that Cobb rejects? What is meant when Cobb writes, "The Christian might assume that because there is only one reality the dialogue partner and the Christian must be experiencing the *same aspects* of that same reality" (p. 5, emphasis mine)? I believe this sets up a straw man for destruction. The vocabulary is one of analogy with no established technical definition, and is therefore arbitrarily chosen and left to the analogical imagination of the reader. Yet it seems quite obvious that sameness of aspect is precisely what no one claims, and that its leading to "*identity* of insight" (p. 5, Cobb's emphasis) is manifestly absurd. It is not at all clear that Cobb has addressed a position heard in current attempts at inter-faith or inter-tradition dialogue. Is there a seriously held position here which differs from the point of departure stated on p. 4? When on p. 6 Cobb argues for seeing the "foci of the two traditions . . . as compatible without being identical," I believe the same point is in order. If by foci he means God and Emptiness it is rather obvious that they are not identical, and much more needs to be discussed before it is clear what is meant by compatibility in this context. And when this has been conscientiously pursued, it cannot be universalized as a basis for all types of inter-tradition dialogue.

A further point which I find well taken and helpful in Cobb's initial essay is the emphasis on the relationship between faith, trust and willingness to risk dialogue. Likewise, I commend the attention to the relationship between dialogue, persuasion and conversion. I agree that the anxiety to engage in friendly dialogue has sometimes obscured the fact that just as one must be open to wider horizons and new glimpses of truth for oneself, so one must act on the assumption that the dialogue partner is likewise open, and that there is the possibility in both directions not only of the widening of existing horizons from the established vantage point but also of a crossing over to another vantage point. Clearly, we shall present the truth we see as the truth, even while conscious that it cannot be the whole truth, the absolute truth, unconditioned by our particular cultural, linguistic, historical and personal bias.

Among the points that I find helpful in the initial essay by Swidler is the question as to who may dialogue claiming to stand for or speak for a given tradition. The question is most pertinent. I have found in all of my own experiences of inter-faith dialogue, as well as in experiences of Christian-Marxist dialogue, that the answer is not by many means clear or easily established. There are, of course, many informal dialogues taking place in which nothing matters beyond the stance that the individuals themselves take. And there are formal dialogues, often looking to some defined outcome, in which the officially recognized governing or representative bodies appoint delegates to speak for the tradition. Yet in these, as well as in less formal encounters, I have often found that there is a reluctance to accept that lay persons might speak for Catholicism or Judaism, for example. Swidler's solution may be the only possible one, but the problem continually returns to haunt us, the more so as many traditions experience cultural change and variety and their members respond to continuing dialogue and coexistence with members of other traditions. The concern to encounter the orthodox Catholic, or the authentic Hindu, or the Jew with a proper Talmudic outlook, may become less and less appropriate to the reality of people's lives and experience in these communities.

Connected with this is a reservation I have concerning Swidler's initial statement. To say that those who are sure of an absolute hold on the truth cannot dialogue because they are not open to learning, implies a narrower definition of dialogue than I like to employ. I believe there can be a genuine dialogue simply for the purpose of information and mutual understanding of positions. I may be convinced that Christians have a hold on the truth of divine revelation absolutely and yet, because I live in Pakistan, be courteously and genuinely curious to know and understand as much about Muslims and their religion as possible. I may do it as a matter of diplomacy, to avoid awkward and dangerous mistakes, or I may do it as a matter of courtesy and sensitivity to avoid doing anything offensive, or I may do it because I am interested in the people and want to understand them as much as I can, or simply because I am passionately curious to know about everything about me and particularly interested in the architecture and design of mosques. But in any of these cases, there is much gained, even though I may not expect the knowledge to have any impact on my own religious stance and convictions. Certainly we are all better off knowing one another's religions with some accuracy and depth than we are in relationships largely based on ignorance or distortion.

On the other hand, I do agree with Swidler that in proportion as our expectations and intentions for dialogue are more far-reaching there must also be greater openness to being changed in one's own stance and vision of reality. In that sense, therefore, it is surely true that the gradual post-Enlightenment withering of our claims to absolute knowledge and certainty has opened a moment of opportunity for deeper and more far-reaching dialogue with persons of other faiths and convictions. Moreover, I am in solid agreement with the contention Swidler makes that the fulness of dialogue with others is something more than merely intellectual but involves many dimensions of experience.

In the more practical suggestions the other three initial essays have proposed, I find many good ideas, and nothing to disagree with. If dialogue among persons of different faiths and positions is desirable, then obviously many and various attempts to accomplish it in different contexts with varying partners are also desirable, and the more such attempts the better. In fact, in the matter of practical initiatives it is not as helpful to prescribe as to describe what has been done and seems to have been fruitful for those concerned and possibly for a wider circle of beneficiaries.

In relation to the hermeneutic of restrictive texts, there may be more to say. With Knitter's application of his soteriocentric christology to Acts 4:12, the "no other name" claim, I find I can agree that the intent seems to have been immediate, practical, contextual, and not universally exclusive of other peoples, in other times and places and cultures, from salvation. The matter may, however, be more complicated, if the ecclesial use of the quotation throughout the Christian centuries were to be examined closely and with reference to the various contexts.

Cobb's interpretation of John 14:6, the "way, the truth and the life" text, interpreting the "I" of the saying very broadly as the Logos inclusive as it were of the *logos spermatikos* in all history, is certainly not an impossible interpretation. I do find it extraordinarily broad even in the context of John's Gospel with its resonant symbolism. Whether the interpretation is permissible may depend a good deal on what is seen to be the relationship of John's Gospel to the rising tide of Gnosticism.

Swidler's Johannine text, John 1:1,14, the identity of the Word with God and the incarnation of the Word, is closely related to the above and Swidler's interpretation is also closely related to, though not coincident with, Cobb's interpretation. In this case the continuity with Hebrew thought about the self-expression of God, and the possibility of understanding the Johannine imagery within that tradition, is more readily evident. I find myself in substantial agreement with the interpretation Swidler gives. Here again, it is not the hermeneutics of the biblical text that I see as complex or problematic, but the analysis of the ways in which the tradition of the Christian churches has quoted, interpreted and used the text in its continuing and developing statements of doctrine, including those which have in the course of time become central and obligatory elements for Christian theological reflection.

As I reflect on the initial exchange of essays, my dominant thought is that a great variety of approaches really is possible, because there is a great variety of different purposes for which dialogue may be undertaken, a great variety of people who may enter into it, a great variety of occasions and situations, as well as different ground appropriate to the particular traditions that are represented in a particular encounter. The kind of dialogue that appeals most to me is the kind that asks: what do you seek by your religious quest or practice? What do you find helpful or even necessary in your quest? What are the obstacles you find in the course of your quest? Do human suffering, wars, famines, oppression and such problems relate to your quest? Does your religious understanding offer hope for the solution of such problems? What do you think of us who do not share your religious vision and stance? Can you pray with me? Can I pray with you? Can you collaborate with me on practical projects, and if so, what kind?

All these are the questions that I find of primary interest, though they lead to further questions, such as: What do you believe? How do you think you should act? What, if any, are the forms of your worship or religious observance? How do you explain your worldview? How do you designate what is ultimate for you? But these, I think, are secondary questions.

Response I

—

Leonard Swidler

I have come to this "Dialogue on Dialogue" with what I think is a dialogic attitude, that is, I came *primarily* to learn from my partners. At the same time, I presumed they came with a similar attitude, and therefore I have also written down my understanding of interreligious, interideological dialogue as one essential part in this learning conversation. I will leave it to them to decide whether or not they have learned anything so far in this encounter, but for my part I can say that I have indeed learned a great deal – and look forward to learning still more in our conversation.

One, I have found many prior agreements among my partners, and between them and myself. That is very encouraging, for it leads me to think that I, we, are in those instances not all that far from an accurate grasp of reality. Given the fact that very many of those ideas arose from relatively new perceptions, insights and convictions, certainly for me, and I know for at least some if not all, of my partners as well, it is a real gain to be thus confirmed and encouraged.

It is clear to all of us that in taking positions strongly in favor of interreligious, interideological dialogue we have had to confront a great deal of resistance within our various communities – perhaps especially the Catholics among us, although no one can forget that the Protestants have their own resistant element in the Fundamentalists. Hence, it is deeply reassuring to be made aware once again that we do not walk alone.

Two, I have also learned new insights. It would make no sense to repeat them all, of course, but let me mention just one as an example of how, at times at any rate, new insights arise.

In John Cobb's discussion of the citation from the Gospel of John which has Jesus saying, "I am the way, the truth and the life; no one comes to the Father except through me," which traditionally is understood exclusivistically, his presentation of the context was simplicity and clarity itself – hence its effectiveness. He wrote that if one is interested in finding the historical Jesus, it is to the pages of the Synoptic Gospels that one must turn in the search. However, he noted, presenting the historical Jesus was not at all what John was interested in. Rather, as he put it, "The Jesus of John is the Jesus of faith, the Jesus of the imagination of the early church, shaped of course by memories of historical events but more by the living experience of Christ in the community."

Now in the past I had thought, read and even written similar things myself, but I had not come across its expression in this simple, clear, "of course!" form before. As a consequence, my understanding of that very important, influential New Testament situation has thereby been clarified, deepened. And so it was with a number of other insights newly gained in this dialogue so far, and so it will be with all authentic dialogues.

Three, I have likewise had some previously held positions modified by this encounter so far. The most dramatic example has to do with Paul Knitter's plea for making human liberation the necessary entry point into interreligious, interideological dialogue. However, because I want to "complicate" that example by also offering it as an instance of my fourth category, I will put off dealing with it until a little later in this response.

Four, in some instances, I want to offer some additions, and even at times alternate approaches and wording, to what some of my partners have said. Here is one example of an additional remark:

Monika Hellwig, in introducing the third way of responding to exclusivist religious claims – that is, looking for the questions underlying scriptural and/or traditional texts that have most often been understood in an exclusivistic manner – said that it is "more convincing within the community of faith." And she is right. I would want to add that this new hermeneutical analysis can be fruitful in providing new insights and a possible basis for dialogue with outsiders only if it is undertaken (as she has done) with what in my initial reflections I called a "deabsolutized," relational, understanding of truth-statements.

To the extent that this "deabsolutized," relational, understanding of truth is assimilated and Hellwig's new hermeneutical analysis is successfully pursued, individual believers, and eventually whole institutions, can pass through a prior stage of faith development to a more mature one, wherein it becomes apparent to them that there are ways of perceiving reality and understanding its meaning in an integrated manner other than their own.

There has been some important research in this area that can be applied to the issue of interreligious, interideological dialogue which I would like to reflect on here. In this connection it is helpful to note that there is a relationship between an individual's cognitional, moral judgment and faith-ideology development, and that these relationships have been worked out by pioneer scholars such as Erik Erikson, Jean Piaget, Lawrence Kohlberg, and James Fowler.

Lawrence Kohlberg and his colleagues developed a schema of three pairs of stages of moral judgment development; he calls them "preconventional," where the standard for moral judgment tends to be the self; "conventional," where the standards come from the outside society; and "postconventional," where the standards tend to go beyond societal patterns to general principles.[1] (It should be noted also that in all these various advancements, the attainments of the previous stages are not rejected, but are taken up into the next higher stage and transformed.) James Fowler, building on the work of Jean Piaget and Kohlberg and adding to it that of Eric Erikson with his emphasis on the psychosocial dimension of human development, has built an impressive body of field research and analysis, on the basis of which he formulated his theory of six stages of, now not moral judgment, but faith-ideology development.

What have special bearing here on interreligious, interideological dialogue are the characteristics Kohlberg and colleagues have found in what they call the postconventional stages, stages five and six, and what Fowler and colleagues have found in his stages five and six of faith-ideology development (faith, as used by Fowler, clearly is not restricted to "religious" faith, but includes all grounding explanations of life, i.e., religions and ideologies).

Kohlberg comments on the move from conventional to postconventional moral reasoning as follows: "The rejection of conventional moral reasoning begins with the perception of relativism, the awareness that any given society's definition of right and wrong, however legitimate, is only one among many, both in fact and theory."[2] This in fact is a deabsolutized, relational view of truth, which, I am convinced, a person must have even to be open to, let alone be capable of, engaging in interreligious, interideological dialogue. Thus it appears necessary for a person to have begun to move to Kohlberg's stage five in moral reasoning in order to engage in authentic interreligious, interideological dialogue.

In writing about his stage five in faith-ideology development, Fowler has some strikingly pertinent things to say:

Stage 5 accepts as axiomatic that truth is more multi-dimensional and organically interdependent than most theories or accounts of truth can grasp. Religiously, it knows that the symbols, stories, doctrines and liturgies offered by its own or other traditions are inevitably partial, limited to a particular people's experience of God and incomplete. Stage 5 also sees, however, that in the relativity of religious traditions what matters is not their relativity to each other, but their relativity – *relat*-ivity – to the reality to which they mediate religion. Conjunctive faith [Fowler's stage 5], therefore, is ready for significant encounters with other traditions than its own, expecting that truth has disclosed and will disclose itself in those traditions in ways that may complement or correct its own. . . . Conjunctive faith's radical openness to the truth of the other stems precisely from its confidence in the reality mediated by its own tradition and in the awareness that that reality overspills its mediation. The person of Stage 5 makes her or his own experience of truth the principle by which other's claims to truth are tested. But he or she assumes that each genuine perspective will augment and correct aspects of the other, in a mutual movement toward the real and the true.[3]

Again, it would seem clear that Stage 5 faith-ideology is a prerequisite of authentic interreligious, interideological dialogue. Before that, interreligious, interideological encounters would be prolegomena to authentic dialogue.

The age pattern of the appearance of Stage 5 faith-ideology also has a bearing on this issue. According to Fowler, transitional Stage 4–5 does not appear until the twenties, and then only in relatively small numbers when covering the whole spectrum of US society (on the average before then there has not usually been sufficient life experience to provide a base for attaining that level of maturity). However, of those adults over thirty that his team interviewed in depth (359 persons – half of them male and half female and from a wide variety of educational, economic and social backgrounds – over eight years), a third of them attained transitional Stage 4–5 or higher, meaning that a third of the US population (assuming the sample is as truly representative as Fowler and colleagues tried to make it) over thirty is capable of authentic dialogue.

It should also be noted that with higher levels of education the percentage of more advanced faith-ideology stages proportionally increases. Since, by the very nature of the enterprise, those persons most likely to be interested in interreligious, interideological dialogue will also tend to have higher than average education levels, the percentage of relatively highly educated Americans above thirty who are open to participating in interreligious, interideological dialogue because they are at Stage 4–5 faith-ideology development (and hence capable of authentic dialogue) should be considerably higher than 33% – just how much higher (40%? 50%? –%?) is not known since the necessary statistics are not available.

The fact that this is clearly not the case suggests that the churches, synagogues, mosques, temples and other religious institutions tend to operate and attempt to hold their membership to a much earlier stage of faith development. Fowler in fact does judge the Christian churches and the synagogues to be operating at a much earlier, more restrictive stage:

The modal developmental level is the average expectable level of development for adults in a given community. . . . The operation of the modal level in a community sets an effective limit on the ongoing process of growth in faith. My observations lead me to judge that the modal developmental level in most middle-class American churches and synagogues is best described in terms of Synthetic-Conventional faith [Stage 3,

ideology-centered, that is, "we are right, therefore, the others are wrong"]
or perhaps just beyond it.[4]

What of the more than 33% of the over-thirty population of the US who
are at transitional 4–5 stage or higher? Have they left the churches and
synagogues, are they often frustrated and underutilized by them? If they were
mostly present and active and not restricted, it would seem there would be a
great deal more creative interreligious, interideological dialogue occurring
on the grass-roots level and above than there seems to be. What of those
church and synagogue members at Stages 2 and 3 who are held back rather
than encouraged to advance to their full capabilities? The potential for good
within the churches and synagogues is immense; the actuality is much less so.
Might the situations in other Western religions and ideologies, e.g.,
Marxism, be similar (my experiences in Christian-Marxist dialogue certainly
lead me to say, yes, for the latter)?

What the facts are in non-Western cultures, religious and ideological
traditions requires careful work; the importance of such work for interreligious, interideological dialogue, for theology, for ideology, for religions in
general, and human life on this globe can hardly be overemphasized.
Fortunately Fowler and his colleagues are beginning seriously to investigate
his findings and analyses cross-culturally.

What also needs even more research and thought is the correlation
between stages of faith-ideology development and interreligious, interideological dialogue on the level of the group and the culture. Bernard Lonergan
raises the issue when speaking about the educational process,

> in the difference between the child beginning kindergarten and the
> doctoral candidate writing his dissertation. But the difference produced by
> the education of individuals is only a recapitulation of the longer process of
> the education of mankind, of the evolution of social institutions and of the
> development of cultures. Religions . . . all had their rude beginnings,
> slowly developed, reached their peak.[5]

One need only think of the official stance of the Roman Catholic Church
toward dialogue with non-Catholic Christians, let alone non-Christians,
before Vatican II and after. The former was vigorously negative, and the
latter just as vigorously positive. Vatican II was clearly a conversion
experience on the level of a whole religious institution, and it was equally
clearly based on the attainment, officially, of a new level of cognitive capacity,
which allowed the institution also to advance to Stage 5 in faith development.

Again, one need only do a comparative study of the Vatican documents in
regard to the limitations on absolute claims resulting from an awareness of
history, or in regard to the possibility of learning from other religions, both
before Vatican II (e.g., Mortalium animos, 1928; Humanae generis, 1950) and
during and after. The transition from Stages 3 and 4, ideology-centered, to

Stage 5, dialogue-oriented, is very apparent. Of course the implementation of the official transition has been anything but smooth and painless; the resistance on the part of those Catholic officials in positions of power who personally have not yet themselves made the transition is intense.

Let me move on to a point where rather than just making an addition I would like to suggest other wording. John Cobb wrote that "we cannot have dialogue without confrontation," and added that of course confrontation must be supplemented by dialogue. I would like to suggest nuancing the use of the term confrontation in this connection. It is true that there are situations when dialogue is not the proper response to someone, but rather, confrontation, or, opposition, as I wrote. That response, however, is usually restricted to cases where we understand evil is being perpetrated. Now it is also in fact true that in situations less "critical" than these people often do engage in confrontation, and then nevertheless sometimes eventually do move on to dialogue. However, I wonder whether this move is because or in spite of the confrontation. I think the latter.

John Cobb, and Paul Knitter and Monika Hellwig as well, also speak of "persuading" as an essential part of dialogue; Knitter even wants to place persuasion (or witness, or even "conversion" of a particular sort, as he put it) first. I believe I understand what they all are trying to say with this term. Partly, I believe, they wish to argue that dialogue does not mean simply presenting oneself as a blank slate upon which the partner can write whatever s/he wishes, which one will thenceforward hold as one's own position, but rather that one comes to the dialogue with convictions, just as one's partner does, and that both try to persuade each other of the validity of their positions. They also want to say that if one is convinced of the truth of something, that means one holds that position to be universally true, and hence feels responsible for informing, convincing, persuading one's partner that that position is indeed true – otherwise you would not be holding it! – and that therefore s/he should also hold it; to do less would be a disservice to one's partner.

As is clear from what I initially wrote, I too believe that I should come to the dialogue as I truly am, that is, with a number of firmly convinced positions, which I should not simply give up or cover over. I too am convinced that many of the things I hold to be true have a universal quality about them, that is, that they are true for everybody. However, some nuancing is needed in this universal claim when we are speaking of the *meaning* of something, for then clearly "I," with all my perspectival particularity, am essentially involved in the articulation of the "truth statement" and obviously its universal applicability is thereby diminished.

Further, I believe that we will run into "psychological" difficulties if we come to the dialogue with the assumption that confrontation is a proper starting point or that persuasion is an essential part of dialogue, let alone the first part. My understanding of what fundamentally makes dialogue different from other kinds of intellectual encounters is that each partner comes to the encounter *first of all* to learn. If I come to teach, to persuade, then all the old, familiar-over-the-centuries resistances will come forth, and the likelihood is that not only will no one learn, but also, correspondingly, no one will persuade. I come to the dialogue because I want to *learn*, and change accordingly. If I want (especially, first of all) to persuade, I don't go to a dialogue, but to a debate, an argument, a teaching situation, or the like. Again, of course I come to the dialogue convinced that I have truth – but not all truth, and it is the truth that I do not yet know that I am seeking to learn in the dialogue.

Dialogue, like all authentic human acts, starts out with a proper *self*-love, with which I can then "love my neighbor *as* myself." The different religious and philosophical traditions are replete with utterings that say basically the same thing, starting with the various forms of the "golden rule" found in most religions. Scholastic philosophy put it thus: *Nemo dat quod non habet.*

Confucian thought is especially pertinent in this instance. For Confucianism the essential human act is learning to become human; the question then is whether this learning to be human is to be done "for the sake of others (*wei-jen*)" or "for the sake of self (*wei-chi*)."[6] The Harvard University Confucian scholar Tu Wei-ming points out that theoretically learning to be human can be done for both reasons, but that although learning for the sake of others may appear altruistic, Confucius criticized it as inauthentic: "A decision to turn our attention inward to come to terms with our inner self, the true self, is the precondition for embarking on the spiritual journey of ultimate self-transformation. Learning for the sake of the self is the authentic way of learning to be fully human."[7] Translated to the question of "Why dialogue?" the answer is, first of all for my sake, so *I* can learn.

This starting with a proper *amour propre* also provides the basis on which to act concerning those truths which we are convinced we already have when we enter into the dialogue. On the one hand, in dialogue, rather than trying to persuade my partner of something, I try to explain my understanding of it as clearly as possible precisely within that particular dialogue context so as to clarify *for myself* my understanding of the matter under discussion – for my understanding will constantly be in need of rearticulation as it is constantly related to new insights, experiences, questions that arise in the dialogue.

On the other hand, also in dialogue rather than trying to persuade my partner of something, I try to explain my understanding of it as clearly as possible as a *quid pro quo*, that is, as a response to my partner, who *also* comes to the dialogue primarily to learn – and to be able to do so I must explain the matter in question as clearly and intelligibly as possible, just as s/he did for me. Thus, again the movement is in what I see to be the proper order, and with the proper motive – from love of self to love of neighbor.

Since we all nevertheless seem to be in fundamental agreement in this area, this may seem like unnecessary quibbling, but I think it is important to be as clear and accurate as possible about the terminology and the order and motive of the actions in dialogue, especially for those who will be reading our reflections on dialogue but will not necessarily have had our experiences of dialogue.

Earlier in this response I mentioned that I found a previously held position of mine had to be modified by what Paul Knitter had to say about making human liberation the necessary entry point into interreligious, interideological dialogue. I found enlightening and convincing his argument that the four contemporary critical areas in desperate need of *global* (the really operative word here) liberation (physical suffering, socio-economic oppression, nuclear holocaust and ecological catastrophe) must be addressed by all religions (and ideologies) if they are to have any credibility in any sphere in the future. In fact, as he pointed out, the major religions of the world are, to a greater or lesser extent, beginning to address those issues, and partly as a result are also entering into cooperation on them. Without a doubt, the growing awareness of these *global* threats provides a basis, indeed, an impulse, even a compulsion, for the religions and ideologies to enter into dialogue and cooperation.

That all religions and ideologies ought to have a commitment to these global liberations – yes! That such a commitment will lead toward dialogue and cooperation – yes. That this commitment "would be *the* [emphasis added – but implied] starting point . . . for dialogue" – I don't think so.

As the earlier Christian ecumenical movements (e.g., "Life and Work" *and* "Faith and Order") bear out, "liberation praxis" surely is *an* authentic way to enter the dialogue. But besides this "practical" way there have been, and are, *de facto* also other ways to enter interreligious, interideological dialogue, e.g., the cognitive, spiritual, esthetic. Why must the practical be the only proper way to enter the dialogue? Is it not rather a matter of circumstances, psychological inclination, talents, state, and stage, in life, and many other things, that in fact lead individuals and groups into dialogue?

Let me be even more specific, in response to Knitter's specificity. He gives the clear impression that he wants to make the entry ticket into authentic interreligious, interideological dialogue be a commitment to socio-economic liberation (basically with a "liberation theology" agenda, utilizing the well-known phrase, "preferential option for the poor" – to which he elsewhere adds, "and the nonperson").

I confess that at times I feel somewhat uneasy about this urging. To be sure, structures of dominance must be unmasked and dismantled wherever they are to be found, and that demands a constant searching within and without. But, at the same time, it is important to be aware that it is not possible for the "haves" in a material sense to eliminate the material poverty of the "have-nots" simply by "external" changes, such as by modifying the social structures, or heavier taxes, or lowering their own material standard of living. Some, or perhaps even all of these and more, are doubtless necessary, but they are not sufficient.

It is not mainly in the direction of "giving up things" on the part of the "haves" that the "poor," and "nonpersons," will be liberated, but rather in the direction of doing more, both qualitatively and quantitively. We have learned in the last two centuries that material wealth is not limited, static; it is essentially linked with "spiritual wealth," with mental creativity, which is dynamic, unending. It is essentially, though not only, this latter, spiritual wealth, that needs to be expanded, shared; the former, material wealth, will then follow. This lesson is being learned today, the hard way, by such Marxist countries as Hungary: "Our existing socialism had to realize that *structural changes* either in the economy or in the very society itself *do not involve automatic changes in the mentality* of the people."[8]

Along this line Hungary is now even inaugurating a multiple party political system! – and also Poland *de facto* – and Gorbachev with his *perestroika* and *glasnost* is likewise desperately trying to get that giant Communist country to learn the same lesson.

I would like to suggest that the "Other" toward whom our "altruistic" ethical action should reach might be named simply the oppressed, the *unfree*, in any dimension – and who is completely free? Logic, of course, also directs that those in greatest need should receive the greatest attention, but it likewise directs that each person should contribute according to her/his gifts, and in a pre-eminent, though not exclusive, way to those before them *now* in need, whether that need be material, spiritual, social, esthetic, or whatever: producing good material things both for the well-to-do as well as the poor, teaching both the poor as well as the well-to-do, making democracy work better both for the well-to-do as well as the poor, creating beauty both for the poor as well as the well-to-do. In the US, for example, the material poverty of the 30 million "poor" must be eradicated, but at the same time the various spiritual poverties of the 220 million "well-to-do" must likewise be diminished. This *"preferential option for the unfree"* in no way rules out the "preferential option for the poor." Rather, it includes it – in eminent fashion – but expands it.

It seems to me that the question of timing is also all-important. Both Christianity (as well as other religions) and Marxism have in practice far too often sacrificed the present generation to both the past and the future. Because of its age, Christianity has been much more guilty than Marxism of sacrificing the present to the past (tradition!), but both have been equally guilty of sacrificing the present to the future: Christians have often been taught to accept their lot as God's will, not to try to change the social structure of things but to look forward to a future reward (popularly expressed: Pie in the sky bye and bye). Populations in Marxist countries have often been told that they ought not to try to change the economic order of things but to give up "consumer goods" so future generations could benefit from their development of "heavy industry" (leading to their present economic mess in which neither consumer goods nor heavy industry are adequately developed).

Here again, Marxist Hungary has been learning this lesson the hard way (but it is learning it!): "What is more, individual persons are not only citizens to be governed, but also autonomous living beings with specific needs and rights. Their basic needs and rights cannot be neglected for a long period without considerable damage even to society, and in consequence to the state. . . . The socialist system in Hungary aimed to achieve social justice. . . . But in the recent past the fact had to be faced and acknowledged that *a new type of poverty* emerged: . . . *in the financial sense* . . . *in a moral and human sense* . . ."[9]

Without diminishing in the least the burning need for the "haves" of this world – largely, though by no means only, Christians and Jews (or in short, the "First World") – to move out from their *amour propre* to a commitment to socio-economic liberation, I believe it is also important for all to remember that until very modern times life for the vast majority (that is, in the magnitude of 90%!) of the people of the world was, as Thomas Hobbes said, "nasty, brutish and short." It is only with the advances of the West in science, medicine, economics and social/political structures that there could even be a Third World as differentiated from the First World. (In many ways much of the "Second World," that is, the Communist world, is really Third World in its economic and socio/political underdevelopment, which it too is now admitting and beginning to try to overcome.) Until modern times the whole world was what we today call Third World.

Hence it does not make sense to accuse the present First World of having *created* the Third World. What does make sense is to call on the First World to move from its appropriate, indeed necessary, prior love of self to its appropriate, indeed necessary, continuance of the act of love to the Other. For not only can I not love my neighbor if I do not love myself; I also cannot truly love myself if I do not also love my neighbor. In fact, I become an "I" only in encounter with the Other. In the social, economic, political spheres, that means that the First World must strive to "do unto others as it would have them do unto it," that is, cease policies and practices that worsen or continue the underdevelopment of the Third World and, rather, facilitate an ever more human social, economic, political reality for the Third World, and thereby also for itself.

To this the religions (and ideologies) of the world should be prophetically committed, both singly and jointly. Clearly when it is the latter, that will lead to dialogue, and dialogue will in turn lead to and reinforce individual and joint action, and both will lead to a deeper interiorization, which will again stimulate the other two areas – and so on endlessly, in a foretaste of and participation in infinity.

Notes

1. Lawrence Kohlberg and Carol Gilligan, "The Adolescent as a Philosopher: The Discovery of the Self in a Postconventional World," *Daedalus* 100 (Fall, 1971), p. 1072.

The work of Kohlberg is to some extent challenged by his co-worker Carol Gilligan with her argument that he did not take women into account in his surveys. See, Carol Gilligan, *In a Different Voice*, Cambridge: Harvard University Press 1982. However, that problem does not arise in the work of Fowler, for his interviews are fifty-fifty women and men.

2. Ibid.

3. James W. Fowler, *Stages of Faith*, New York: Harper & Row 1981, pp. 186f.

4. Ibid., p. 107.

5. Bernard Lonergan, *Collection*, ed. by F. E. Crowe, New York: Herder and Herder 1967, p. 254.

6. Confucius, *Analects* 14, 25.

7. Tu Wei-ming, "On Confucian Religiousness," paper delivered at the International Confucian-Christian Conference in Hong Kong, June 8–15, 1988 (pp. 7, 8, 16) – a revised and enlarged version of chapter five, "Centrality and Commonality: An Essay on Confucian Religiousness," in his forthcoming book, *Centrality and Commonality: An Essay on Chung-yung*, to be published by the State University of New York. William Theodore de Bary, *Neo-Confucian Orthodoxy and the Learning of the Mind-and-Heart*, New York: Columbia University Press, 1981, p. 21, also documents thoroughly that this is indeed the position of Confucius and the Confucian tradition.

8. Laszlo Lukacs, "Changing Forms of Religiosity in a Changing Society," a paper prepared for a Christian-Marxist dialogue between Americans and Hungarians in Budapest, June, 1988, to be published in Leonard Swidler (ed.), *Human Rights: A Christian–Marxist Dialogue*, New York: Paragon 1990.

9. Ibid.

Response II

—

John B. Cobb, Jr

We all agree that we are remarkably close together. Whether this is an advantage or a disadvantage overall is a valid issue, but it is an advantage at least in that the critical questions addressed to me reflect basic understanding of what I want to communicate. Accordingly, they are astute and pertinent. My task in response is not so much to defend what I have said as to improve my formulations and advance my thinking.

I was particularly startled by Hellwig's charge that the position I opposed was a "straw man." Since she herself seems to exemplify the position I was intending to criticize, my first reaction was to dismiss the criticism, but on reflection I realized that she was correct. The way I described the position I had in mind does not accurately identify any seriously held view!

The problem is with the word "aspect" which I used repeatedly and which she quotes. To speak of different aspects of reality means to speak of different ways in which an identical reality is apprehended. I opposed the view that all religious traditions focused on the same aspect of reality. Hellwig is correct that no serious thinker supposes that reality is apprehended in just the same way by all traditions. I am indebted to Hellwig for having pointed out my mistake. The word "aspect" simply does not mean what I intended by it!

Having acknowledged my error, let me try to state better what I meant to say. Reality in its totality contains many interrelated parts, entities, principles, elements, realities, ultimates, etc., and I mistakenly used "aspects" as a shorthand way to refer to all this. What I meant to say is that different religious traditions in some instances have the same part, entity, principle, element, reality, or ultimate in view, while apprehending this differently, and in some instances have different ones in view. Hellwig correctly notes that my sensitivities on this second difference have been shaped especially in dialogue with Buddhists. I have reacted against the effort to show that the biblical God and Buddhist Emptiness are two ways of apprehending one and the same part, entity, principle, element, reality, or ultimate. Since that effort is still widespread, what I *meant* to criticize is not a straw man.

My view is not that what Buddhists name as Emptiness has played no role in other traditions. On the contrary, it is the same reality that Hindus call Nirguna Brahman, and this is sometimes referred to as Godhead or Being Itself in the West. These different terms, arising in different traditions, out of different experiences, have led to quite divergent ways of apprehending the common principle, element, reality, or ultimate.

In a similar way, I believe that Judaism, Christianity, and Islam all focus on one part, entity, principle, element, reality, or ultimate. Further, Buddhism attests to this also in its interest in Amida, and various Hindu groups have strong theistic tendencies. What seems important to me is to decide in each case whether representatives of different traditions are expressing differing apprehensions of one and the same part, entity, principle, element, reality, or ultimate, or whether they are focusing on different ones. (The reader may understand why I used the one word "aspect" to avoid this long recital, misleading though it is!) Dialogue is possible and valuable on both bases. But the nature of the discussion differs.

I emphatically do not propose that these personal hypotheses generated in the course of dialogue should become prerequisites for dialogue. My concern is rather that prerequisites for dialogue should not be so formulated as to exclude my views from the dialogue. When dialogue among religious traditions is supported on the grounds of a commonality inherent in religion, very often this exclusion occurs. Is it not better to allow persons with different views to enter dialogue with open minds on this question?

Hellwig rightly notes that the relation of God and Emptiness needs much fuller discussion. I have written on this subject elsewhere and hope that in part I have provided the discussion needed, but that still more is needed is no doubt true. In any case, she is correct that insofar as I have universalized the pattern of Zen-Christian dialogue to all inter-tradition dialogue, I have erred. I hope I have not done that. My conviction is that we should enter each dialogue with open minds to *discover* what is shared and what is disputed between us. On the other hand, she is right that my dialogical experience has led me to certain overviews and hypotheses that are different from hers. I have pointed to some of these hypotheses in the preceding paragraphs. I have been led to think that Jewish-Christian dialogue is quite different from Buddhist-Christian dialogue. As a hypothesis with which I enter dialogue, or even encourage others to do so, I do not see that this need be harmful.

Hellwig grants that my interpretation of John 14:6 is "not impossible," but she is not sure it is "permissible." That could lead to an interesting discussion of what is "permissible." If only that interpretation is permissible that exactly reflects the conscious intention of the original writer, I think we are all in trouble. First, we will never know. Second, much was in the mind of the original writers that cannot be appropriated in our changed situation and worldview. I have little doubt that the writer was engaged in polemic with Jews of his day who rejected the Christian claim about Jesus. He may have intended to deny them any access to God. But surely what is not permissible for us as Christians today is to continue the polemical use of this verse. If the original meaning of the verse were exhausted by polemical intent, we would be forced to preach against it in the name of the Christ to whom it witnesses. But obviously this is not the case. The verse is also a powerful expression of the heart of Christian experience. In Jesus Christ we find the way, the truth, and the life. There is, we believe, no other way, truth, or life by which one could come to the Father. But whatever that statement meant to the one who first uttered it, for us it cannot mean that Jews do not participate in this way, this truth, and this life. And in the canonical form of the Gospel we are given the way to understand that not only Jews but all people participate in that way, truth, and life that we find uniquely incarnate in Jesus. I need more help from Hellwig to understand why this may not be permissible hermeneutic today.

Swidler is so generous in his response that my inclination is just to say thank you and go on. But he does raise one concern, and even though there is nothing that he says on this topic with which I disagree, it may be worthwhile to say a little more. I have emphasized the role of confrontation, and this makes Swidler uncomfortable for good reason. "Confrontation" sounds, and can easily be, arrogant, complacent, insensitive, and destructive. It can prevent dialogue rather than initiate it, or enrich it.

Nevertheless, I do want to stress what I take to be important and valuable in confrontation. I can use our own dialogue about dialogue as an example. Hellwig confronted me. My response is, no doubt, partly defensive, and to that extent not very valuable. But she also brought me up short, forced me to recognize mistakes and inadequacies, pushed me to think further. I am grateful for her confrontation. In response I have also confronted her. There is, of course, danger in such confrontation. One of us may take offense and withdraw from conversation. But nothing in her confrontation of me evoked such feelings on my part, and I hope that I have not offended her in such a way that she would not want to continue the discussion. There are still points on which I would like to understand better what she is saying and others on which I would try further to persuade her to accept parts of what I propose. To me this seems healthy.

In Swidler's response I do not find myself confronted. Of course, I am gratified by his generous statements of appreciation. I have also learned from that. I will try in future not to move so quickly to points of disagreement. But because he does not confront, or, if at all, confronts me so obliquely, I am not drawn into further reflection.

It is not only in this context that confrontation seems to me valuable. It has in fact played a crucial role in inter-tradition dialogue as well. Probably the most important confrontation thus far has been the Jewish confrontation of us Christians with our collective responsibility for the Holocaust. Of course, in confronting us with that, Jews took a great risk. We might have reacted primarily with anger and defensiveness and hardened our anti-Judaism. That kind of backlash is still possible. But thus far, the primary result has been to stimulate extensive rethinking on the part of Christian theologians. How can we reformulate our received traditions so that they will function to generate positive appreciation of the Jewish community and its traditions rather than the enmity that has characterized Christians for nineteen centuries? Much remains to be done, but real progress has been made. Without harsh confrontation, I fear that little would have happened.

Whether Christians are in position to confront Jews is another issue. Clearly most of us are not. Only those who have truly repented in the deepest sense of *metanoia* have earned the right. Even they must ask whether the time is ripe. Nevertheless, in principle, I do not believe it is healthy to avoid confrontation altogether. Judaism is far from perfect. Certainly it is primarily the responsibility of Jews to deal with its imperfections, just as it is primarily the responsibility of Christians to deal with the imperfections of Christianity. But for Christians to fail to tell Jews what they miss in what they see in Judaism does not lend itself in the long run to healthy dialogue. Further, there are practical outcomes of Jewish thought to which it is wrong for Christians to be oblivious. Compared with the Holocaust they pale into comparative irrelevance, but suffering is suffering even when it is on a smaller scale and does not have genocidal implications. Close to the heart of Jewish faith are beliefs that are encouraging excesses in relation to Palestinian Arabs. A few Christians, such as Rosemary Ruether, have, in my judgment, earned the right to say so and are exercising that right. Our goal as Christian partners in the dialogue should be to become the sort of Judaized Christians who *can* confront as well as, again and again, be confronted. Until then Jewish-Christian dialogue will be incomplete.

In other dialogues, the obstacles to confrontation on our part are less acute. Sharing as I do Knitter's commitment to dealing with the most urgent issues in the world today, I find myself increasingly confronting Buddhist friends with the limitations of their responses. This is not for the sake of persuading them to join Christian churches, but for the sake of encouraging movements already occurring within Buddhism. For example, I have supervised two dissertations by Buddhists on Buddhist social ethics, one from the perspective of Zen and one from the perspective of Pure Land. I think both are excellent contributions to the creative transformation of Japanese Buddhism. Since I believe that creative transformation is Christ, I see myself in this work as a servant of Christ, but I do not ask that Buddhists think of this in that way.

Swidler and I are not far apart. He is rightly convinced that the first steps toward and in dialogue normally require a primary emphasis on listening, especially from the Christians involved. He thinks that given the whole history of Christian imperialism, an emphasis on confrontation is just what most Christians do *not* need. To confront without having first listened and learned would only continue age-old patterns against which we are all in needed reaction. I only want to add that in the course of dialogue it is possible to develop sufficient trust that confrontation is possible, and that until that element is included the dialogue is incomplete.

My dialogue with Knitter has a long history. It has focused on the one question of whether there must be a common ground among all religions on which dialogue is based. His identification of that common ground has changed from time to time, and his openness to the depths of variety has grown, but that both parties in dialogue need to enter the dialogue for the same reasons seems to be an unshakable conviction on his part. Since I do not agree, the argument continues.

This time Knitter argues that all of us are "presupposing some kind of commonality among the religions – a commonality that transcends doctrinal expression or ritual – ethical practice." He deduces this "from the fact that we all believe that religious believers engage each other in order to foster understanding (at least), agreement (at best), and cooperation (at last)." At a certain level, Knitter is surely correct on all this. I, at least, agree that these are worthy purposes of dialogue and that dialogue partners have something in common. Nevertheless, I find Knitter's formulation once more misleading.

It is true that "religions have *in common*, some shared context or basis." All human beings do, whether they are religious or not. Dialogue is possible between physicists and biologists, between socialists and capitalists, or even between biologists and capitalists. Christians can have dialogue with any of these groups. Certainly that means we share a common planet and a common humanity at some level. If this were all Knitter meant, there would be no problem. But if this were all he meant, I doubt that he would be preoccupied with the matter. If all human beings share this, he could take the prerequisite for dialogue for granted, as I do. But since Knitter continues to argue the point, it seems clear that he is asserting more than the obvious. He seems to be arguing that religions *qua* religions share something more than this and that it is this "more" that grounds their dialogues. I fear that he also means that parties to dialogue need to agree on what this "more" is *before* they can engage in dialogue. For this "more" he provides no evidence, and for elevating this "more" into a precondition of dialogue he gives no reasons. I wish we could agree that the only precondition of dialogue is the willingness to engage in it.

Knitter thinks that he finds me also laying down additional conditions. He rightly notes that I doubt that Christians holding to certain theologies are likely to share my enthusiasm for dialogue. That implies, he thinks, that certain beliefs are required in distinction from others. He certainly has a point. I do believe that among Christian theologies some lead to desire for dialogue more than others do, and that some are likely to lead to unwillingness to engage in dialogue with persons of other Ways. But I do not see what is gained by erecting those beliefs most conducive to dialogue into preconditions of dialogue. If those Christians with beliefs very different from mine find reasons in their faith to engage in dialogue, let us rejoice. It is not for us to tell them that they do not share the prerequisites for dialogue.

Although I certainly favor understanding and cooperation and see certain types of agreement as also playing a positive role, I would not formulate the major reason for Christians to engage in dialogue in Knitter's way. I want to be changed. In relation to Jews it is certainly good to understand them, to cooperate with them on appropriate activities, and to identify areas of agreement. But these gains pale in significance beside that of reformulating Christian teaching and biblical hermeneutic so as to change the total impact of Christianity on the attitudes of Christians toward Jews. It is the change of Christianity that I seek in dialogue. I call the kind of change I seek "creative transformation." If I thought the goals of dialogue were only those Knitter lists, dialogue would have a much lower priority for me.

Knitter knows that I do not fit well into his consensus statement. I deeply appreciate his sensitive probing of what I have written intended to show that my position is not, after all, so different from his. He presses me to clarify my intentions and to think further. He rightly notes that there is in my thought a strong impulse to go beyond contradictions and oppositions, and he thinks this is close to what he intends by commonalities. I think the basic difference between us is that he seeks to identify already existing commonalities in advance of dialogue and to make their acceptance a precondition of dialogue. I, on the other hand, favor beginning wherever we are, clarifying within the dialogue, and then working toward a more comprehensive vision in which the deepest insights of both sides are reconciled.

I favor this *for Christians*. My discussion in this volume has to do almost entirely with Christian participation in dialogue. I have not tried to say what Muslims and Hindus seek in dialogue. Of course, I as a Christian hope they will be creatively transformed, but I am open to the possibility that there is no inner impulse within Islam or Hinduism to submit to such transformation. That is for them to decide. I would prefer that they decided it in the course of dialogue, but if their traditions require that they predecide this before entering dialogue, then I will join the dialogue on that basis. I will still try to open myself to creative transformation and I will confront them with my conviction that much is missed if they refuse to do so. But I will respect their negative decision all the same. I will *not* make acceptance of my goal on their part a condition for initiating or continuing dialogue; and I will hope to learn from them what their goals are. Perhaps that will change my goals as well.

With these further specifications of my views, I will try to respond to Knitter's questions. He asks: If I do not affirm any specific commonality of religion as a starting point, why do I say that "it is a serious mistake to accept incompatibility as final?" My answer is that in one sense of the terms I am a realist and a rationalist. That is, I believe that reality is as it is, including, but not exhausted by, all sorts of human interpretations. That means that all utterly correct statements about any part of it must be compatible with one another. The problem, of course, is that "utterly correct statements" are on the whole beyond our reach. Most of our statements, when not hopelessly vague and confused, are partly correct and partly incorrect, or correct with unspecified qualifications. These partly correct statements often contradict one another. Some people have decided simply to accept such contradictions as final. My view is that the ultimate goal is so to qualify the contradictory statements as to render them non-contradictory – and, ideally, coherent. For example, eventually I hope that quantum and relativity theories can be rendered non-contradictory and even be integrated. I believe that when that happens the statements uttered by physicists will be likely to be more nearly correct than at present. As long as contradictions remain, I see them as a sign of unfinished work.

I hold the same hope for the relation of religious and scientific statements. They are often so very different that the issues of contradiction hardly arises. But there are points of contact at which the issue does arise. When contradictions appear, I see this as an occasion to re-examine statements made on both sides with the goal of avoiding contradiction and even attaining coherence.

That I have the same commitment with respect to statements made by Jews and Hindus does not, therefore, imply any special view about commonality among all religious traditions. I do believe that all religious people along with any who are not religious inhabit the same universe. I do believe that completely accurate statements about any parts of this universe, as explored in diverse traditions, cannot contradict one another.

I have another hope and expectation: that is, that on the whole communities are most strongly attached to those features of their systems of belief that have best proved themselves in experience. This may not *always* be the case, but it is hypothesis with which I approach dialogue partners. I expect my partners to be more flexible and yielding on some of their formulations than on others. When conversation moves to the nub of the matter, I expect there to be a confidence that, however inadequate every formulation may be, there is something profoundly real or true to be expressed. I have referred to these points as their deepest insights, and I hope and expect that these deepest insights will not contradict my own – however different they may be. My goal will be finally to integrate these insights with others I have received from my own tradition.

Knitter is certainly correct that these are assumptions and hopes with which I approach dialogue. I know that dialogue may never proceed to the point where they will be finally vindicated, but some progressive vindication does occur in many discussions, including inter-tradition ones. We have all repeatedly found that verbally contradictory statements, when fully explained, turn out to be making different, but not necessarily mutually exclusive, points. My argument is only that even when contradictions do not readily yield to such resolution, we should be slow to assume that they never will. At the very least, I want to remain clear that my very best formulations are always, and will always be, provisional, so that their contradiction by the formulation of deep insights by another will always function as a challenge to revise.

I need to qualify all this once more. I find it difficult to believe that any of the great religious ways of humankind are simply wrong in their deepest convictions. But there may be religious people and even religious groups whose central affirmations are perverse and destructive and from whom there is very little to be learned. Being religious does not guarantee that one has genuine insights.

Knitter warns that the pluralism I advocate can be dangerous. It can lead to a tolerance of positions that oppress the poor and degrade the environment. He is correct, and whether I have guarded sufficiently against that is hard for me to judge. I have tried to emphasize the role of confrontation to indicate that the appreciation of plurality is not a passive tolerance of what I judge to be evil. But in any case, his formulation of my position shows that I have still not made my real point clear.

In emphasizing that there may be (I believe, is) a plurality of ultimates (I hope I have *not* said "absolutes") that have attracted attention from religious people, I do not mean that those oriented to each should simply live and let live in relation to those oriented to others. That is what "pluralism" means to many. My call is for change, creative transformation, at least of Christians. I have argued especially that Christians can be creatively transformed as they learn from Buddhists. I hope for creative transformation for other traditions as well, and I have argued that Buddhists can be creatively transformed through interaction with Christians. But even after such mutual transformation, there will be differences. Hence plurality will not disappear, and new opportunities for mutual transformation will emerge. But I hope that none would any longer blind themselves "to the conflict, injustice, or oppression that lurks below the surface of such diversity." What I want to bracket is neither the content of what I find supremely important, for example, that we transmit a habitable planet to our children's children, nor the conviction that this is important for all, but only the opinion that it is *more* important for all than what others regard as supremely important. *Perhaps* becoming empty is just as important! In any case, once I am persuaded of its importance, even if not of its *equal* importance, I am inwardly driven to clarify the positive relations between preserving the biosphere and becoming empty rather than assuming that one *must* be subordinated to the other. But if I cannot reconcile them, I will remain chiefly concerned for the future of the planet and confront my Buddhist friends with the danger (even if they do not perceive matters in this way) that exclusive attention to becoming empty individually may inhibit urgently needed actions.

Finally, Knitter wants to know how, if Jesus Christ embodied the truth of the everlasting Word with unique "fullness," this truth can be supplemented. Knitter's critique is well taken. To speak of supplementing what is already full is, at best, confusing. Yet I do not want to give up my point. John's prologue distinguishes between the way the Word functions as the light that enlightens everyone and the way the Word functions as it becomes flesh. I spoke of its becoming flesh as its appearance in unique fullness. That is poor language. In *Christ in a Pluralistic Age* I described the structure of Jesus' existence in terms of his "I" being co-constituted by the Word and his personal past. This is the doctrine of incarnation that lay behind my unsuitable language. To believe that in Jesus the Word is uniquely incarnate does not mean that all the wisdom that has come into being through the Word's presence in all people is available in Jesus. Even if we restrict ourselves to knowledge *about* the Word, this remains true. What we know of the Word in Jesus is dependent on what was already known of the Word, and it is supplemented by what we have come to know through subsequent reflection.

In conclusion let me thank all my colleagues for a stimulating dialogue. I hope that we have modeled as well as discussed good dialogue. Inevitably, we break off in the middle. All dialogues do.

Response II

—

Paul F. Knitter

These two rounds of responses seem to follow the pattern that John Cobb outlined in his opening statement: In Round I, after having listened to each other and determined large areas of commonality, each of us *confronted* the others with our own differing, critical viewpoints. In this round, our conversation goes deeper as we try to *respond* to, learn from, and perhaps be *transformed* by the differences between us. I for one found the differences expressed in Round I to be just as intriguing as the similarities in our initial essays. For me, these differences are by no means peripheral footnotes to a common vision. They touch on key issues that determine just how realistic our shared vision of interreligious dialogue is and how it can – if it can – be carried out.

Personally, I found myself shaken, sobered, and sometimes confused by the way my colleagues have "confronted" me. In other words, I have experienced real dialogue. What hit me hardest was the suggestion made by all three – explicitly by Cobb, more softly by Swidler and Hellwig – that I have fallen into the very "sin" that I have over the past decades been preaching against: that of exclusivism, or more sharply, imperialism. Having swept my house clean and driven out the demon of exclusivism (by questioning whether there really is "No Other Name"), I find that seven other such evil spirits have reentered my dwelling!

I have been told that with the model I proposed in my opening statement, I end up excluding people from the table of dialogue, or I impose my own conditions on them before I allow them to sit down. If I am hearing my colleagues correctly, they are telling me that such exclusivistic or imperialistic tendencies stem fundamentally from my inordinate need to lay out too many conditions – or to establish too much common ground – for the dialogue before it actually begins. They pointed out that such tendencies are embodied in two forms: (*a*) trying to clear the table of all absolute claims before the conversation starts (here I find a fellow-sinner in Swidler), and (*b*) insisting that we begin from what I have called a soteriocentric basis. In other words, after all my haranguing in years past against "absolutes," I end up making absolutes out of non-absolute truth and out of liberation. The demons have returned!

From friends, one can hear such strong, yet gentle, criticisms. In what follows, I hope to make clear how my colleagues have brought me to change my mind, but also how they have helped me to speak more carefully and clearly. I don't think the seven devils have yet returned, but my colleagues have certainly showed me how they might – and what I must do to make sure they don't.

Making non-absoluteness into an absolute

Both Cobb and Hellwig are uneasy, to say the least, when Swidler and I urge participants in dialogue to loosen their grip on "traditional understandings of uniqueness" and on claims to have the absolute truth or revelation. Cobb contends that such preconditions for dialogue are exclusionary in that they tell people, especially conservatives who may be eager to dialogue, that "they 'cannot' approach the table of dialogue without first passing through a theological conversion" by which they renounce their claims of absolute uniqueness (Cobb, p. 82). Such preconditions would not allow believers to "affirm and celebrate the uniqueness of Christ, of Christianity, of the Qur'an, of Krishna, of Buddha. To surrender any of these in their uniqueness either as a condition or as an outcome of dialogue seems to me a loss to be keenly regretted" (ibid.). In support of Cobb, Hellwig suggests that absolute claims do not necessarily impede conversation, for they still allow "a genuine dialogue simply for the purpose of information and mutual understanding of positions . . . [without any] impact on my own religious stance or conviction" (Hellwig, p. 101). For different reasons, Cobb agrees, pointing out that the claim to have an absolute truth does not mean that "one supposes oneself to be in possession of all truth worth having. Many of those who think that they have *some* absolute truth still acknowledge that more is still to be learned" (Cobb, p. 82).

And so, rather than place any restricting conditions on participation in interreligious conversation, Cobb and Hellwig want to promote a totally open table. We should not "campaign for some one way of doing things" (Hellwig, p. 99). "There is really a great variety of approaches possible . . . the more such attempts the better" (p. 102).

Cobb's and Hellwig's admonitions are, I have to admit, on target. We do spend too much time preparing for dialogue, dissecting its nature and the conditions for its possibility, when such efforts would be better undertaken within the dialogue itself. And especially when these preconditions are laid out according to a typical liberal agenda, they can be discriminatory. As another critic has uncomfortably pointed out:

... Hick and many other contemporary philosophers of religion [and theologians like Swidler and Knitter] claim to want to foster a universal religious dialogue, but it turns out that evangelical Christians, Hasidic Jews, traditional Muslims, and so on are not really eligible to join that dialogue, because they will be unwilling to accept the proposed rules of the game, rules that seem to emerge from a modern, Western, academic tradition.[1]

Perhaps the whole issue of absolute truth-claims and whether they are an impediment to genuine conversation should simply be set aside, at least before or during the initial stages of dialogue. The topic is too delicate and seems to touch the very identity of religious persons.

But to table this issue of religious truth-claims does not mean that it will go away. And this is where I would respond to Hellwig and Cobb that sooner or later, if interreligious dialogue gets under way and takes its course, the issue of traditional understandings of the uniqueness of Christ, the Qur'an, etc., are going to have to be faced. Notice, I am speaking about *traditional* or generally given understandings of absoluteness and uniqueness. When Cobb describes absolute truth to mean that I have some and you have some, he seems to contradict, I think, the usual or traditional meaning of absolute. The "absoluteness of Christianity" has generally meant, in words used by Karl Rahner, that in Jesus Christ Christians have been given a revelation that is *superior* to, *normative* for, *unsurpassable* by, *definitive* to all other truth. This is the understanding of "absolute" and "unique" that, sooner or later, will stymie dialogue – at least as soon as the conversation moves from the mere sharing of information (a necessary but not the ultimate intent of dialogue) to feeling the impact of another religious claim on my own.

Therefore, when I stated that religious persons with such absolute claims "cannot" participate in dialogue, I was making a *descriptive*, not a prescriptive, statement; the "cannot" meant not that they are "not allowed" but that, as far as I can understand, they are "not able." I certainly would not want to exclude them from the conversation table, but once they sat down, I would eventually want to ask them – or in Cobb's terms, "confront" them with – the question how they can really play the game of dialogue when they have been given all the trump cards by God. In fact, I would have to ask John Cobb how even his "minimal condition" for dialogue of "listening respectfully" can be fulfilled if Christians approach dialogue convinced that whatever they hear can be true and meaningful *only if* it conforms to the definitive and normative word of God in Jesus. I do not think such listening is respectful of the other; in fact, I do not think it is really listening at all. Cobb has not made it clear, at least to me, how such common understandings of the absoluteness and finality of Christ are *not* an impediment to dialogue.

When he states that "a Christian convinced of the superiority of Christianity can profit from dialogue with a Hindu equally convinced of the superiority of Hinduism" (Cobb, p. 83), I would suggest that this would *not* be the case if the

Christian or Hindu is convinced of the *absolute* superiority of her/his religion
– as Christians have been. If I am open to the possibility that *some* Christian
teachings are superior to those of Hinduism, whereas *some* of the Hindu
beliefs are superior to those of Christians, then dialogue can take place. But if
I believe (as most Christians have always believed) that whatever truth might
exist in Hinduism has ultimately to conform to the final, definite norm of
Christian revelation, then all we are left with is sharing an understanding of
our differences. I will never really allow myself to be challenged by something
in Hinduism that is genuinely different from my Christian beliefs. And if I
cannot do that, I cannot really dialogue.

Here I think I have different expectations of dialogue from Hellwig.
Ideally, it should move from sharing information to being challenged and
possibly changed by the genuine otherness of my partner; but when that starts
to happen, any "absolute claims" get in the way. Therefore, I have to agree
with Swidler that if religious dialogue is really going to take place, the
participants, perhaps not before but within the dialogue, will have to move –
or better, they will find themselves moving – to *something like* Fowler's fifth
stage of faith development; they will recognize or discover that theirs is not
the only or the final or the normative religious truth. (Feminist and class-
conscious critiques of Kohlberg and Fowler, however, have left me
profoundly skeptical about the neatness of these stages of development and
the overly rational process of moving from one to the other.)

But having said all this, I would implore John Cobb please to try to
understand that I can still join him in "affirming and celebrating the
uniqueness of Christ and of the Qur'an, and of Krishna and Buddha." I
realize now that it was perhaps a mistake for John Hick and me then to title
our recently edited book *The Myth of Christian Uniqueness*,[2] as if we were
denying the uniqueness of Christ and Christianity. Rather, we wanted to urge
that assertions about the uniqueness of Jesus, like all symbolic and mythic
language, have to be understood carefully, and reinterpreted often. When I
and other Christians following the so-called "pluralist model" for interreligious dialogue question the uniqueness of Christ, we are trying to reinterpret
it, not deny it.

Such a reappropriation of what it means to say that Jesus is unique might
follow the lines recently suggested by Edward Schillebeeckx (who, it seems,
has thus revised his own christology). The uniqueness of Jesus does not
necessarily mean that Christian revelation is *absolute* and *final*, but it does
mean that God's Word in Christ is *universal and indispensable* for all peoples.
The uniqueness of Christ in regard to other traditions, therefore, means
universality, not *finality*; the Christian Word is vitally meaningful for all
peoples of all times, and not to have heard this Word is to have missed a
"saving" vision of truth; but it does not mean that this Word is the normative
fulfillment of all other Words. Indeed, this understanding of Christ's
uniqueness as universal but not final recognizes a possible analogous

uniqueness (universal and indispensable for all peoples) in the "revelations" (a Christian term!) contained in Buddhism, Hinduism, Islam, African religions, etc. There would be a possible complementary uniqueness among religious figures and traditions.[3] Such an understanding of the uniqueness of Christ allows – rather, demands – a full personal commitment to Christ on the part of Christians; but at the same time, it allows a genuine openness to what God may be doing in other traditions.

I believe it can be shown that such a reinterpretation of uniqueness is consistent with the New Testament witness.[4] But as Hellwig has reminded us, a revision of such texts, though valid in itself, cannot dispense with a revision of how these texts were understood and used throughout ecclesial history and teaching. This is a typical, and necessary, Roman Catholic reminder. For the moment, all I can say is that the revision of creedal or magisterial statements about the uniqueness of Christ can follow the same tack as the revision of New Testament texts. Indeed, Hellwig herself has followed such a tack in her analysis of the Athanasian creed in her first response: the primary intent of such claims about the uniqueness or superiority or normativity of Jesus and the Gospel was to call Christians to a greater commitment, not to denigrate or castigate other religious figures or religions. Today we are called to be faithful to this primary intent, not to the literal meaning.

Making liberation an absolute

The criticism that touches the heart of my suggestions (and my own heart and personal concerns) is that I have turned a concern for liberation and human-ecological well-being into an absolute that either excludes or subordinates other approaches to dialogue. Both Swidler and Cobb urge me to "cool it" and to recognize that dialogue can start with or focus on a variety of concerns depending on context or personality. Again, Cobb warns me of the dangers in proposing "*the* right way to engage in dialogue" (Cobb, p. 80). He also cannot see much of a difference between my rejection of a common *foundation* for dialogue and my proposal for a common *starting point* based on a soteriocentric core within the religions. In proposing a global context of common problems and concerns for human-ecological well-being, I try, according to Cobb, "to define the common context and have agreement on the definition as the basis for dialogue about how to respond." And for Cobb, this is "a new form of imperialism" (Cobb, pp. 8of.). Both he and Hellwig ask what I would do with religious persons – Cobb suggests a Hindu as an example – who do not share this concern for worldly well-being. Have I not fashioned another "precondition" that will exclude them from the dialogue?

Again, I have to admit the validity of my colleagues' questions and warnings. They point out inadequacies and unclarities in what I have proposed as a soteriocentric model for interreligious encounter. In my sense of the urgency of having to respond to the cry of oppressed people and the oppressed earth, I may have proposed a liberation-centered dialogue in a way that excludes or devalues other methods. That was not my intent. When I said that I wanted to *propose* not *impose* this approach, that also meant I did not want to *oppose* others. I see the relationship between a liberation-centered model and other models as one of *integration*, not opposition. As the Roman Catholic bishops of Asia, reflecting Swidler's suggestions, have stated, there are various forms of dialogue that must be distinguished but cannot be separated: the dialogue of understanding and study, the dialogue of prayer and shared experience, and the dialogue of life addressing the issues of the day.[5]

But while I recognize that there is "no one way" for going about dialogue, I also want to propose that a concern for the suffering and victims of the world *must* be integrated into all other forms of dialogue. Though modified, this is still a strong claim. So I want to make it respectfully, carefully. In fact, I would follow Cobb's advice: "Can we not approach dialogue with an open mind, allowing our partners to define their starting points and their goals and then reflecting together on whether they are the same or different?" (Cobb, p. 81). In approaching dialogue and in listening to the starting points of others, I want to propose that a religious dialogue that in some way, at some point – not necessarily, I admit, at the beginning – does not include a concern for and a commitment to overcoming the widespread oppression and suffering in our world is somehow incomplete and inadequate.

In fact, to be honest, I want to press my proposal even further: a concern for human and earthly welfare is not only an element that must be *integrated* into other concerns, but it deserves to be given a certain *priority*. Even though we may not always start with a concern for oppression and suffering, it can serve as a focus for our study and our prayer and further reflections. I urge such a "preferential option" for the suffering and oppressed for two reasons: (*a*) the *practical* reason that, as I tried to state in my initial essay, it can serve as a hermeneutical method that will facilitate dialogue and other methods of dialogue: it will enable us to understand each other and to pray or meditate together more effectively and meaningfully; but also, (*b*) the *moral* reason that the degree of suffering and the threats to peoples and to the planet are such that every religion, as it reflects on its central teachings and core experience, will feel the obligation to respond. This brings us to the issue of a common starting point based on a soteriocentric core in the religious traditions of the world.

I think there is a difference between what so-called anti-foundationalist philosophers criticize as a *foundation* for crosscultural discourse and what I have called a common *starting point* or "shaky common ground" for dialogue. The term "foundation" is used to indicate an absolute position or criterion, existing outside the fray of historical limitations and human discourse, that can serve as the means for knowing the truth and deciding between conflicting truth-claims. Such foundations, in the experience of many, do not seem to exist. What I mean by a common starting point or context would be a set of issues or concerns or even values that are agreed upon *in* our conversation and then serve as guidelines or criteria for understanding and evaluation in the further conversation. When I stated that I "trust that . . . differences [between religions] are unitive rather than separative," I was not suggesting, as Cobb seems to have misunderstood, that there is a uniform foundation grounding all the religions but that they can agree on such a body of common concerns about the well-being of peoples and the earth.

I certainly do not want to define this common context so as to dilute the real differences in the ways the various religions understand both cause and remedy for the common problems of world hunger, oppression, nuclear threat, and ecological havoc. Here I think Cobb simply misunderstood. A liberation-centered dialogue will thrive on such differences. But the thriving will be possible on the basis of common commitments to common, global concerns. Such concerns can, I think, be found among representatives from all religious traditions, as Cobb himself recognizes when he admits that "all religious traditions have some idea of the wrongness" of the global issues we have been talking about. (Cobb, p. 81).

This is what I meant by a "soteriocentric core" within the religions – a core of beliefs and values – different in each religion! – because of which significant numbers of devotees will feel themselves obligated and empowered to respond to issues such as hunger, exploitation, nuclear war. In stating this, I do not naively imply that every follower of every religion brims with a this-worldly concern for the welfare of humanity. One has only to look at many Christians to disabuse oneself of such naiveté. I am suggesting, however, that within the sacred scriptures and the mainstream traditions of what are called the "world religions" as well as of the "primal religions," there is a concern and a commitment – expressed in vastly different ways – to promote human well-being and betterment in this world. Therefore, within all the world religions, we can find *some* – I would make bold to say, *many* – believers who would not only willingly endorse but cagerly embrace what we are calling a salvation-centered (or this-worldly) context for interreligious dialogue.

I *trust* that such a soteriocentric core exists within each tradition. But I also see mounting evidence that it is being identified or "retrieved" by representatives of most of the traditions. One can speak of "theologies of liberation" arising throughout the religious world. A recent example of the kind of dialogue that can result when the differing soteriocentric cores are linked took place in fall of 1988 in the dialogue-seminar on "Liberation, Religion, and Culture" sponsored by the Asian Cultural Forum on Development, held in Ayutthaya, Thailand. This meeting assembled fifteen participants representing the major religious traditions of Asia, including Buddhism, Christianity, Hinduism, Islam, and indigenous religions; they came together to share their experiences on the liberative dimensions of their respective traditions.[6] A similar meeting of twenty-five Buddhists, Christians, Muslims, and Hindus from Third World countries met in Colombo, Sri Lanka, in August 1987, and issued a moving final statement entitled "Opting for the Poor: The Challenge to the Universal Religions."[7]

I am not saying that dialogue can take place *only* among such groups, but I am saying that it can and should take place *especially* among them. Therefore I would certainly not refuse to talk with Cobb's Hindu friend, whose "deepest insight" has nothing to do with this-worldly liberation, just as I would not refuse to speak with my fellow Christians of similar persuasion. But I would *confront* them with the moral appeal which not just I but their own co-religionists are voicing that the Gospel or the Bhagavad Gita requires us to be concerned about those who are suffering. And if they refuse to admit such concerns into our interreligious dialogue, I would, to be honest, search out other Hindus who do have a concern for the victims and the victimization of this world. I would prefer a dialogue with other believers who share a preferential option for the oppressed, not because I disdain other-worldly believers or feel they have nothing to say to me, but because a liberation-centered dialogue seems to me to be both more urgent and more promising. And I would hope that there will be a time when I can return to the dialogue with those who do not share this preferential option.

Finally, also in regard to my proposal for a soteriocentric interreligious dialogue, Swidler raises some objections to claims I never made. ("Me thinks he doth protest too much"!) He reminds me that we cannot bring about socio-economic change simply by changing external structures (I never said we could) and that a concern for material poverty should not replace a concern for spiritual poverty (I never said it should). Swidler goes on to claim that the root of the problem and of the solution is spiritual: "It is essentially, though not only, this latter, spiritual wealth, that needs to be expanded, shared; the former, material wealth, will then follow" (Swidler, p. 112). I'm not at all so sure! Such an assertion might have a hard time standing up against the evidence of history. One can look back, for instance, at centuries of Christian missionaries sharing their spiritual wealth with Latin Americans – without too much material wealth following along for the masses of indigenous peoples. For similar reasons, I would also have to disagree firmly with Swidler's suggestion that we cannot blame the First World for the problems of the Third World. "Until modern times the whole world was what we today call Third World . . . Hence, it does not make sense to accuse the present First World of having created the Third World" (Swidler, p. 113). Again, I don't know how historically accurate that is. I think a case can be, and has been, made that the precolonial economies of, for example, Central America and Africa were far more propitious to the masses of people (though, of course, there were class differences and corruption) than what happened after the arrival of the European colonizers.

Certainly, if radical and lasting socio-economic transformation is going to be realized in the Third World (including the third worlds that are present within USA society!) there will have to be more than structural change and a simple redistribution of wealth. But I would strongly contend that there will also be no real differences for the masses of the poor without structural change, sometimes revolutionary structural change; nor will the problems of the Third World ever be solved unless there is a more just sharing of material wealth – read, control of the international economy – on the part of the First World. At least, this is what I am hearing from my liberation-centered dialogue with Buddhists, Hindus, and Muslims of the Third World.

I was moved and challenged by Cobb's closing image of the table of dialogue as one of "open communion." And I hope I have learned from him and Hellwig and Swidler how to keep myself from "fencing" the table. (There is more for me to learn, I know.) Certainly, open communion must be our ideal. But just as I have slipped into making absolutes out of non-absolute positions and out of a concern for liberation, so also there is a danger of making an "absolute" out of openness. This might be one of the lessons of the Gospel parable in which *everyone* is invited to the table of the wedding feast, but once they get there they are expected to have a wedding garment (Matt. 22:1–14). There are dangers in absolute openness, or in a resolve to "keep the conversation going at any price." Such admission of everyone and such delighting in more and more differences can turn out to be a distraction or an excuse for not responsibly taking positions on some of the intolerable realities in our present world – positions which would require us to resist, perhaps dissociate ourselves from, others. As Simone de Beauvoir has pointed out, a gala celebration of openness and diversity can be "the perfect ideology for the modern bourgeois mind."[8]

So yes, all are invited to the table of dialogue. But I would urge that once we are assembled we must openly speak to, yes confront, each other about what is the "context" of our conversation, and what are the issues and require-ments that make it possible and worthwhile. More specifically, I propose that we must, like Paul and the Corinthian church, remind ourselves that often "our meetings are not profitable but harmful," for as we gather around the table to break the bread of dialogue, there are "divisions" among us and the families of nations and there are many who are hungry (I Cor. 11:17–22).

Notes

1. William C. Placher, *Unapologetic Theology: A Christian Voice in a Pluralistic Conversation*, Louisville: Westminster/John Knox Press, 1989, p. 146.

2. *The Myth of Christian Uniqueness: Toward a Pluralistic Theology of Religions*, John Hick and Paul F. Knitter, eds., Maryknoll: Orbis Books and London: SCM Press, 1987.

3. Edward Schillebeeckx, "The Religious and the Human Ecumene," in *The Future of Liberation Theology: Essays in Honor of Gustavo Gutiérrez*, Marc H. Ellis and Otto Maduro, eds., Maryknoll: Orbis Books, 1989, pp. 182–6.

4. See Knitter, *No Other Name? A Critical Survey of Christian Attitudes toward World Religions*, Maryknoll: Orbis Books and London: SCM Press, 1985, pp. 173–86; also, id., "Dialogue and Liberation: Foundations for a Pluralist Theology of Religions," *The Drew Gateway* 58, 1988, 33–48.

5. See the Final Statement of the Asian Bishops Institute for Interreligious Affairs, 1979, published in the Papers of the Federation of Asian Bishops' Conferences, No. 25.

6. As reported in *Inter-Religio* (Nanzan Institute for Religion and Culture) 14, 1988, 69.

7. See the full text in *Buddhist-Christian Studies* 8, 1988, 189–94.

8. As cited in David Tracy, *Plurality and Ambiguity: Hermeneutics, Religion, Hope*, New York: Harper and Row and London: SCM Press, 1987, p. 90.

Response II

—

Monika K. Hellwig

In the final analysis, people may come to dialogue for a variety of reasons and with a variety of goals in mind, but almost any dialogue is better than none. In this discussion we have stressed various values, objectives, considerations and cautions which arise out of our particular experiences. It would be foolish to suppose that the understanding we have at this point is somehow definitive or normative for others. It is more in the way of something exemplary and suggestive, something challenging and also at points cautionary.

In a shrinking universe, in which populations become daily more mingled, almost any dialogue is better than none, because dialogue is an antidote to the xenophobia from which wars, street violence, persecution and discrimination come. It is best that dialogue with those of other persuasions be friendly, sensitive, and courteously attentive, but even an angry exchange flung over the fence conveys information and affective nuances that enhance awareness of what is important and precious or significant to the others. In relationships between individuals in family life, an angry exchange is often revelatory, and there is no reason that it should not be so in interfaith or interideological exchanges. However, it is not only angry exchanges which may turn out to be, after all, useful. The same might be said of casual exchanges to which we pay little or no attention. That is the way we get to know and understand those closest to us – by constant casual contact and casual exchange establishing a pattern and a profile. In such a way, the mingling with strangers in street or marketplace also establishes a pattern and a profile. This should not be undervalued, although it is necessary to guard against such profiles becoming caricatures.

What this means is that a great deal of dialogue among persons and groups of various convictions and persuasions is constantly going on without being named or recognized. The dialogues that we set up self-consciously are in one sense the tip of the iceberg, but they are also more than that. These prepared and carefully planned dialogues are, among other things, critical sifting and evaluation of the dialogues that go on unnoticed. Moreover, such organized dialogues are an effort to sensitize, to correct any caricaturing that has gone on, to make sure that what is learned of the other is appreciated for its own sake, not used contemptuously or manipulatively. Many specific organizations aimed at structured dialogue have been begun with the intention of correcting prejudices and caricatures, as, for instance, in the case of B'nai B'rith's Anti-defamation League or the Catholic Evidence Guild in England. The limitation of these is that the intent is generally one-sided – to correct misunderstandings about the sponsoring group. Even such cases, however, would seem to be helpful initiatives towards dialogue, because when one side speaks and testifies about itself, the other side, or the various other groups, are challenged to respond. Meanwhile, if any prejudices about any group are corrected, there is progress in living together in the world.

The informal dialogue that continues pervasively wherever people mingle also seems to achieve another benefit. Without much disciplined reflection there is a certain enrichment of one's own tradition and worldview simply from seeing it in contrast and in the context of other traditions. It is contrast that makes objects in the physical universe visible, and this is true also for relationships, values, codes of conduct, social structures and beliefs. Without contrast they are taken for granted, and therefore do not become subject matter for reflection and evaluation. Seen in contrast, they become the focus of attention with the questions "why?" and "how?" and "for whom?" Likewise, in the physical universe, living beings come to visual attention by moving. Analogously, the mingling of peoples brings change, and change calles to attention the state of things that formerly was taken for granted, prompting questions aimed both at intelligibility and at evaluation. Obviously such coming to notice and evaluate elements of one's own tradition is a maturing and enriching process.

What planned dialogue can add to the enrichment of one's own outlook by informal contact with that of others is a sharpening of the focus and a certain legitimating freedom. To become aware, through informal dialogue, of elements of one's own worldview can be a first step. To ask questions about the intelligibility and value and interrelationships of these elements certainly has a further liberating effect. In particular, it helps to see one's own worldview not as an alien product dominating one's life, but rather as a way of interpreting and ordering priorities and perceptions by which one lives and takes control of one's life. But it is not only that reflexive understanding can be a means to owning one's own tradition and becoming a creative, active subject within it. There is also the question of feeling free to do so. The clearer awareness and better understanding that can be gained from disciplined reflection on contrasts with elements of other traditions helps towards this. To know the function and reason for some element in one's own tradition is to have a greater freedom in accepting, rejecting or adapting it to changing needs. From a fundamentalist view within any tradition, exposure and reflection of such a kind are necessarily seen as a danger, but from any other view than the fundamentalist, such exposure to contrasts and reflection upon the sharper awareness of disparate elements can only be a gain.

What is actually achieved, then, by explicit, planned dialogue among representatives of various traditions is not so much an entirely new pattern of relationships as a harnessing of existing relationships into a more disciplined and focused exchange. And the content at either level can really be any topic or aspect that happens to come up and to seem relevant and worth pursuing by the dialogue partners. At the informal level that is what will happen in any case, and patterns and correlations may build up slowly, erratically, partially. At the formal level, choices are made, subject matter is chosen, according to the current or long-term interests of the parties. Whether the choices are well or poorly made, impulsive or well thought out, may not matter as much as would at first appear. If there is a dialogue going on at all, the predominant concerns of the parties will surely tend to keep emerging. As long as the balance of power in the conversation is not too unequal there will, therefore, tend to be a corrective force at work to block some of those projection mechanisms by which we take away the voice of the other by deciding beforehand what the other is bound to say, and then hearing only our own version in what is actually being said. Because there is some pattern of coherence in any worldview, discussion of peripheral matters would seem always, sooner or later, to lead to substantive issues or beliefs and convictions.

Formal dialogue across faith and ideological boundaries has tended in our times to be something that the same relatively small number of people does over and over again, often with the exasperating impression that it does not significantly affect their own communities. The effect on the communities as a whole is certainly likely to be very slow, but as long as the external dialoguers are also in conversation within their own communities the influence must eventually penetrate further into the heartland of each tradition involved. There is no doubt that in the shaping both of individuals and of whole cultures and communities, there is a rhythm composed of phases of differentiation and phases of convergence, phases of consolidation and phases of outreach. It is not to be expected that everyone in a given community will be in a rhythm in which all the waves coincide. Moreover, not everyone is temperamentally or by experience inclined quite the same way. There seem to be personality types who look for unruffled stability in their lives above all else, and personality types at the other extreme who look for adventure and new discoveries above all else. Most of us are to be found somewhere between the extremes, but it means that by personal inclination some are much more likely to engage in conversation with strangers and outsiders of every kind and at every level. There is surely an advantage to the community in the interaction and counter-balancing of these types within a given community.

In conclusion, what may be said about the dialogue among adherents of various faiths and ideologies is simply this: let us do it with interest, respect, courage and humility, and let us continue to learn from it.

Response II

—

Leonard Swidler

One of the things one constantly learns anew in dialogue is how multifaceted the search for truth, for reality, for meaning, is. We think we made a point clear to our listeners, but we don't know that until we hear their understanding of our position. In this exchange we learn how we are projected in the world of our partner's understanding – to some extent. Of course, what our partner brings to the exchange, both in general and at that particular moment and in those particular circumstances may have a small or overwhelming amount to do with the image we cast in her/his mind. And I am speaking here not of biased, polemical partners, but of open, sensitive ones. It is only at the cost of a great deal of effort, openness, sensitivity to others and ourselves and self-reflection and struggle constantly to clarify that we can communicate effectively, illuminating the understanding of both ourselves and our partner.

This fascinating lesson is again being driven home here one more time – and I am extremely grateful that it is, for only thus can we painstakingly creep up on an ever fuller insight into and grasp of reality. It is in this context that I take up a few selected themes raised by my partners in dialogue for what I hope will be clarification.

I. Who should dialogue?

One set of questions circles around the general query of who should, or can, be involved in interreligious dialogue. Must one follow all the guidelines for dialogue that I have given in order to participate in dialogue? As I have tried to emphasize here and elsewhere, these guidelines (reproduced in many places and languages[1]) are not my, or anybody else's, *a priori* prescriptions. They are "laws" like the "law" of gravity: if we don't observe it and step out of a tenth-floor window, it will take effect! So too with these *a posteriori* dialogue "laws" to the extent that we don't observe them, to that extent dialogue will not take place; to the extent we do follow them, to that extent we will learn more about reality, and change accordingly – the whole point of dialogue. Thus, these guidelines are both descriptive and hortatory goal-oriented rules – as also are many of the ethical rules of Jesus and other great religious teachers.

Does that mean that if these guidelines are not fully observed, nothing good, nothing dialogic will occur? No, of course not. Most human encounters are not full dialogues, even when they are intended to be such. But even in partially successful dialogues much can be gained and we will all be the better for it. However, it is the very nature of being human that we always yearn for perfection, even though, like the horizon, it always recedes before our striding. And so this expression of the minimal guidelines to be followed in searching for an ever fuller dialogue is offered as an instrument to direct our steps on the never-ending journey toward perfection, not as a set of restrictive statutes.

II. Absolutist and deabsolutist mentalities

John Cobb wonders about the appropriateness of my use of the term of deabsolutized understanding of truth. He says, "The issue is not whether one holds some truth as absolute but whether one supposes òneself to be in possession of all truth worth having." It would seem that we are using the term "absolute" in regard to truth somewhat differently. When I wrote of an absolutized and a deabsolutized understanding of truth I tried to describe *two different mentalities*.

Concerning the first I wrote, "Before the nineteenth century in Europe truth, that is, a statement about reality, was conceived in an absolute, static, exclusivistic either-or manner. It was thought that if something was true at one time, it was always true, and not only in the sense of empirical facts but also in the sense of the meaning of things. This is a *classicist* or *absolutist* view of truth." Thus, in this mentality it is not just human experience and an insight into its significance that is affirmed, but also the particular thought-categories and terminology used that are made the only valid way to describe reality; all other deviant descriptions of the significance of human experience are simply mistaken.

That human experience can be perceived from other perspectives, conceived in other thought categories, expressed in other terminologies, is beyond the ken of this mentality. However, once these other perspectives, thought categories and terminologies are admitted as possibilities, even just minimally and inchoatively, then the move is underway from an "absolutist" to a "deabsolutized" view of truth. The deabsolutized mentality of course does not necessarily eschew affirmations, but it is aware that such affirmations, firm though they may be, are not the only way to perceive, conceive and express that reality, and hence are seen as always limited. Since even our fundamental affirmations are always thus limited, they are always capable of being supplemented, enriched – even if in negatively horrible ways, as we have learned of the essentially destructive thrust of a racist view of human experience from the Nazis.

However, if only those with the mentality of an at least minimally deabsolutized understanding of truth can, or will even want to, enter into authentic dialogue – that is, if only those who realize at least to some extent that because they cannot perceive, conceive and express all truth in their statements, all ultimate reality in their religion or ideology, they are open to and need to enter into dialogue – then what should be the attitude of the "dialogists" toward those who do not share more or less their deabsolutized view of truth?

On the basis of time and energy and pressing need priorities, they might be ignored, but surely not in principle, for that would mean deliberately leaving a possible avenue to a fuller grasp of reality uninvestigated. To make that move on principle would be to fly in the face of the experience of our humanness, that is, our potential openness to all reality, cognitively and affectively. Hence, we will in principle want to enter into dialogue with persons of all other religions and ideologies – at least to the point of truly learning that they are life-threateningly contradictory to our understanding of an authentic human life – at which point we may be compelled to move to opposition, as with racists.

III. Those who do not wish to dialogue?

As I and many others have argued elsewhere,[2] however, a human relationship cannot forever remain one-sided without becoming destructive. Likewise, dialogue cannot forever remain one-sided. If the potential partners are incapable of and uninterested in dialogue because they hold an absolutized view of truth, it would appear that one has but two possible courses of action, other than ignoring them, which in principle is ruled out for the person with a deabsolutized view of truth. It seems clear that the "dialogist" should 1. enter into sympathetic contact with them to the degree possible, not only to learn from them, but also 2. to encourage in them the development of an at least minimally deabsolutized understanding of truth. This latter can of course take place over an extended period of time and in a limitless number of ways.

Given the ineluctably mutual character of a healthy human relationship, if the "dialogist" is in fact in sympathetic contact with "absolutists" and is in fact learning from them, it would seem that this state of affairs could not go on indefinitely without the "absolutists" also beginning to learn from the "dialogists." As that slowly happens, the "absolutists" will proportionately move toward a deabsolutization of their understanding of truth – at first quite unconsciously, but then eventually necessarily consciously (of course, the relationship may be derailed or cut off before this happens). If the mutuality does not develop, then in fact the "dialogists" will eventually begin to cease learning from the "absolutists" and the relationship will gradually slip, at best, into a sort of suspended animation; "at medium," into the old "splendid isolation;" and at worst, into polemics, and possibly even violence. Naturally, in the concrete, situations will not always follow these pure "textbook" stereotypes, but it would seem that they are the built-in tendencies of our human structures.

In any case, those two steps might well be called *prolegomena* to dialogue, rather than dialogue itself, and in many instances they will have to be gone through before authentic dialogue can be arrived at. To affirm so is not to admit defeat, or to be "elitist" (must that always be a bad thing? – I would like to have only an "elite" surgeon operate on me!). It is to take reality the way it is and deal with it accordingly – surely the proper human, religious, way to act.

IV. Contradictions within the tradition

I would like to return briefly to a discussion by Monika Hellwig in her initial statement. When John Cobb takes it up in his response, he agrees with her position and remarks, "Both Knitter and Swidler seem to fall into this trap." My first reaction to Cobb's remark was the proverbial, "I'm glad you raised that question!" The question under discussion is, What, if one is convinced of the rightness of the dialogic mentality, is to be done about the several exclusivist claims in the Christian tradition (other religions and ideologies have analogous ones)? Hellwig offers three possible approaches: 1. see such exclusivist claims as simply mistaken and declare them as such; 2. see exclusivity as a necessary early stage of an institution's establishing its identity, which stage can and should be left behind as maturity is attained; 3. narrow the focus of the exclusivist claim by contextualizing it historiographically, linguistically, sociologically, etc.

Hellwig says that there is a fetching simplicity about the first approach, but it has the disadvantage of needing "to stand above the tradition and judge it," etc., which Cobb quotes, and into which trap he says Knitter and I fall. She makes no comment about the second approach, but *de facto* opts for the third in her exegesis of a quotation from the Athanasian Creed.

I find it a bit puzzling that Cobb calls the first approach a "trap," and that he thinks I have fallen into it. To be sure, there are times in my writing over the decades when I have concluded that certain claims of the Catholic Christian tradition have simply been mistaken. But of course even the official Catholic Magisterium does the same all the time, although it usually simultaneously issues a disclaimer that the now rejected position was ever part of the essential doctrine of the Catholic Church. Thus, the most solemn repeated condemnations of freedom of religion and conscience by Pope Gregory XVI and Pius IX in the nineteenth century were rejected by the Vatican II Declaration on Religious Liberty in 1965; to hold the solemnly declared positions of Popes Gregory XVI and Pius IX today was declared erroneous – though that almost scatological word was certainly not used.

In fact, in my initial statement, when I undertook an analysis of the prologue to John's Gospel which so often has been used to claim an ontological divinity *à la* Chalcedon for Jesus, I thought I tried using Hellwig's third approach rather strenuously: "There is a third way . . . to take particular texts and subject them to an exegetical, hermeneutic and contextual study, to discover what questions they were answering within their own historical, linguistic and cultural setting." She goes on to say that, "in many cases the answer is surprising because texts have been quoted mindlessly out of context in ways that have distorted their original meaning." And that is precisely what I conclude in my exegesis, namely, that concerning the New Testament basis for the Hellenistically conceived notion of ontological divinity of Jesus, "contemporary scholars argue that it is unwarranted."

Now, one may want to dispute my conclusion and that of the other scholars I rely on, but my approach is nevertheless that of the third type. It is true that there is, in my judgment and that of many other scholars, a serious discrepancy between the understanding of writer(s) and first (Jewish) readers of John's Gospel on the one hand, and the authors of the Chalcedonian formula on the other. No doubt it is important to trace the shift from the former basically Semitic to the latter Hellenistic way of perceiving, conceiving and expressing the reality of Jesus.

However, to assume that the two positions must necessarily be compatible, that there is necessarily nothing more involved than a so-called "development of doctrine," is not only unwarranted, but at times it can even be harmful. To use the example referred to earlier, if the movement from Gregory XVI and Pius IX's condemnation of freedom of religion and conscience (calling it *deliramentum*) to Vatican II's affirmation of it can be said to be a "development of doctrine," then the phrase has no meaning, for it cannot possibly be falsified. What kind of change in teaching could possibly not be called a "development of doctrine"? The phrase would become meaningless. Thus, I would want to suggest that all three approaches described by Hellwig, including the first – after the second or third does not completely resolve the antinomy – have appropriate uses.

For example, as a Catholic, it appears to me that it would be very healthy for our institutional psyche to admit that the two above-mentioned nineteenth-century popes, despite their most solemn declarations (and if they were not speaking *ex cathedra*, it again is difficult to imagine what meaning that term could have to an honest scholar, an honest believer), were sadly mistaken on freedom of religion and conscience – children of their time, to be sure, but nevertheless mistaken, just as the Inquisition as a Christian institution was mistaken. We Catholics need to be mature enough, individually and institutionally, to admit that we have made mistakes. In taking this position I am in fact following guideline nine of my own "Dialogue Decalogue:" "Persons entering into interreligious, interideological dialogue must be at least minimally self-critical of both themselves and their own religious or ideological traditions." To the extent that we "fudge" on the honesty required by this guideline, to that extent we will miss the benefit of dialogue.

V. Soteriocentrism and theocentrism

I would like at this point to recall my stress on the primary meaning of the term salvation, coming as it does from the Latin *salus* (*soteria* in Greek), meaning wholeness, health or wellbeing – hence our English words, "salutary," "salubrious," "salute" (to wish good health, as in "hale," from the German "*Heil*," meaning health, healing, from which we get "*heilig*," holy), etc. I noted that, "when we lead a whole, full life, we are holy, we attain salvation, wholeness." Salvation in the sense of being rescued is only a secondary meaning, denoting how we are "saved" from that which endangers our health, wholeness, wellbeing; unfortunately it is largely in this derivative sense that the term salvation has been understood in the Christian tradition since the third century. Christians, and all human beings, need to turn to the primary understanding of salvation, not just for verbal clarity, but as a fundamental orientation for their whole way of life.

Hence, it is a misreading of my intention, and I believe of my writing, to claim that I define salvation "in a rather intellectual fashion," as Knitter does in his first response.

It is important also to note that there is a significant difference between the way I use the term "soteriocentric" and the way Knitter does. For me, the term fundamentally means centering on the fundamental search for *soteria*, "salvation," in the primary sense described above, much as I define religion as "an explanation of the ultimate meaning of life, and how to live accordingly, which is ultimately based on a notion of the transcendent." Knitter uses "soteriocentric" to mean centering on the search for salvation from largely external scourges of humankind, e.g., poverty, nuclear disaster, ecological catastrophe – in other words, an enlarged liberation theology agenda. His is a more sharply focussed understanding of "soteriocentric" as compared to my broader understanding. I would like to suggest that in order to avoid confusion a different term be used for his more narrowly focussed meaning – perhaps "liberation-theology centred," or "social-justice centered?"

All of us humans are searching for salvation, *soteria*, in the primary sense of a whole authentic human life, but how we understand that goal will vary greatly. However, if we recognize both our common starting point and our varying understandings of the goal, we will at once have at hand the joint basis and the needed motivation for dialogue. It is this "soteriocentric" – in the primary sense – basis for dialogue that, in my judgment, ought to be the

general foundation for dialogue among all the world's religions and
ideologies (the latter being "explanations of the ultimate meaning of life, and
how to live accordingly, which are *not* ultimately based on a notion of the
transcendent").

Of course, if our conversation is with fellow theists, then *in addition* to
being soteriocentric it can be theocentric; if it is with fellow Christians it can
yet further *in addition* be christocentric. However, once we have turned away
from staring inward to looking outward, have shifted from monologue to
dialogue – in other words, once we have been literally "converted," "turned
around," we are ineluctably drawn to accept, even seek out, every possible
dialogue partner, for everyone can be a source of a perspective on reality
which is new to us – and for us theists, this is a perspective on Reality. Hence,
I am convinced that once we have made the Copernican turn to dialogue, we
must, consistently, carry it to its widest possible basis: "soteriocentrism."

A last comment about Knitter's use of "soteriocentric" – in his narrower
liberation theology sense, and in response to his "fundamental question for
Swidler". Already in my first response I argued – as John Cobb argued in his
– that though I agreed that all humans ought to be actively concerned and
involved in the global ethical issues he mentions, joint action on them is not
the only legitimate entrée into interreligious, interideological dialogue.
Though for full, authentic dialogue one must eventually engage in dialogue
in all three areas, cognitive, spiritual and practical, I would argue that one can
enter the dialogue through any of the three areas, depending on one's talents,
circumstances, needs of one's "neighbors," and a whole variety of situation
specifics. Moreover, I would ask Paul Knitter concerning his liberation
theology praxis-oriented dialogue the same question that he puts to Hellwig
in his first response: "Is this the only way?" For my part, I think not.

VII. Codes of behavior are not always liberative

In his response Paul Knitter urges Hellwig, and through her the rest of us, to
link together dialogue in the action area with dialogue in the intellectual and
spiritual spheres – to which I say: Amen! At the same time, in the process of
his effort to persuade, Knitter presents the example of certain Asian
Buddhist base communities' application of the Four Noble Truths to their
socio-political problems by which we in a praxis-oriented dialogue can learn
from Buddhist peasants. This is also doubtless true in this instance.
However, I would want to add that it is by no means always true that outsiders
can gain "liberating" knowledge from the way religious ethical codes are put
into action. I believe Hellwig is at least as close as Knitter, if not closer, to the
average reality when she notes that, "While in itself interesting and
important, however, this is not really the best way to get to know the others
because codes tend to establish boundaries rather than highlight the center."
Far too often ethical codes as they are taught and practiced are constricting

rather than liberative; what we can at times learn from other traditions, as from our own, past and present, is what *not* to do: e.g., despising the body, opposition to democracy, fundamentalism, xenophobia. In praxis-oriented dialogue we need to be open, sympathetic and supportive, but also realistic and distinguishing – and willing at appropriate times and in appropriate ways to speak of mistakes when speaking of one's own tradition (as discussed above in section IV), and even when dealing with others' if in the end we find what we judge to be life-threatening contradictions, as analysed in my initial statement.

VIII. Civil/political rights are also the subject of praxis dialogue

I would like to add one further supplementary note to Paul Knitter's plea for the praxis-oriented dialogue. Surely all the liberation theology issues, global and regional, that he speaks of, largely the so-called second- and third-generation human rights, should be the concerns of all human beings, and very certainly those involved in interreligious, interideological dialogue. At the same time I would want to add an equal emphasis on the need for all to be similarly concerned about the so-called first-generation human rights: freedom of religion, speech, association, participation in political decisions, etc. (fundamentally the American Bill of Rights). Just as in the Western world it has been argued – validly, I would say – that there should be no split between civil and political rights on the one hand and social rights on the other, so equally in the East. Moreover, we are seeing in the present day that masses of people in the Second and Third Worlds desperately want those civil and political rights. We need think only of Hungary, Poland, the USSR, Pakistan, the Philippines, South Korea and, most painfully and tragically, China. Those of us living in relatively free societies must never forget that the yearning for freedom is endemic in the human being. Though it can be crushed, numbed, seduced for a time, it will always rise again. It is a human birthright, and must along with the other civil/political rights be included in our praxis-oriented dialogues. Let us strive together in dialogue for the full panoply of human rights wherever there is a human being.

Notes

1. In the form of the "Dialogue Decalogue" these guidelines for interreligious, interideological dialogue were first published in the *Journal of Ecumenical Studies* (Winter 1983), pp. 1–4, and were reproduced at least twenty-nine times in at least eight different languages.

2. See Chapter 2 of my *After the Absolute: The Dialogic Future of Religious Reflection*, Minneapolis: Fortress Press 1990.

Consensus Statements

After our exchanges it is apparent that, despite various differences in terminologies, emphases, and at times even in understandings, we hold a great number of fundamental notions about interreligious, interideological dialogue in common. We wish here to distill out what appear to us to be the most fundamental and obvious of those notions. However, rather than attempt to produce a smooth flowing narrative consensus document – what committee has ever accomplished that?! – we will set down a number of ideas concerning dialogue on which we find we do have consensus:

1. Some of us in our writing here have at times written of conditions, guidelines and the like for "fruitful," "full," "complete," "ideal" interreligious, interideological dialogue, and others of us at times have concentrated on demanding the least possible prerequisites for dialogues so as to make it available to as many as possible. Nevertheless, underneath these differing emphases, we do agree on the basic meaning of interreligious, interideological dialogue, namely, a conversation between partners with different religious/ideological stances in which each comes primarily to listen, and hence learn from, the partner. Naturally, for such listening and learning to take place, each must speak one's own convictions clearly and persuasively, though always respectfully. Implicit in the envisioned listening and learning is change – at the very least in one's attitude toward the partner because s/he now is understood differently, and at the most optimistic in mutual self-transformation.

2. To expand on this point. There are several, graduated, purposes to dialogue. Minimally we hope to gather knowledge about our partner. Beyond that, we seek to learn more about ourselves and our traditions. Still further, if we would act with integrity, we will have to change in light of the new knowledge gained of both the other and ourselves; we will have to embark on a journey of self-transformation.

3. There is a great, and indispensable, value in scholars and leaders of different religions/ideologies coming together for dialogue. However, dialogue is much too important a human activity to be limited to such specialists. Rather, interreligious, interideological dialogue needs to occur with increasing quantity and quality on all levels; if it does not reach the local

level, all the specialists' dialogues – including ours here – will be largely in vain.

4. There are a number of major areas within which dialogue can take place: e.g., the cognitive, esthetic, spiritual, practical (some may wish to refer to this last area as one of "cooperation" rather than "dialogue"). Clearly it is better to have dialogue in just one area, or a few, than in none. However, there is an inner entelechy in dialogue which draws one from dialogue in one sphere to the others, until all have been engaged in. Obviously, for many reasons, not everyone starts at the same point, nor does everyone make the full journey to dialogue in all the spheres with every set of partners, but that inner inclination is structurally there in human dialogue, and optimally it should be consummated.

5. Where we start in a dialogue with a partner will depend on a variety of circumstances, interests, talents, local needs, psychological bent, etc. Thus, we might start in the cognitive, practical, esthetic or spiritual sphere but, again optimally, we should also move on to the other spheres – at a greater or lesser speed depending on many contingencies.

6. In order to engage in dialogue we obviously must hold some things as commonalities and some as differences. Were all held in common, we would have nothing to learn in the conversation. On the other hand, were everything different, we would not even have a language in common with which to have the conversation. Minimally we must have an openness to learning something new; otherwise we would not even wish to enter a conversation.

7. In speaking specifically about interreligious, interideological dialogue we need not, however, claim anything further than the common human search for the meaning of life, and how to live accordingly, that is – in Latin terms – the human search for "salvation," a salutary, whole, healthy life, which of course embraces the inner and outer, the individual and communal person – "soteriocentric" in that basic (this time, Greek) sense. Our understandings of the "meaning of life" can manifest the widest possible divergences, ranging from a total focus on divinity or on inner meditation to complete self-emptying, to being "a person for others" in efforts to transform this world and society, or being a "balanced person" – continuing on in almost endless variety. It is precisely in the sorting through and learning from the underlying commonalities and the persisting differences in our understandings of the meaning of life that the genius and value of dialogue consists.

8. To enter into and benefit from dialogue we can indeed hold certain positions with great firmness, and in that sense adhere to "absolutes" – as, for example: every human has an intrinsic personal worth. However, no understanding or expression of reality can be held "absolutely" in the sense of claiming that the element of reality cannot be perceived and expressed in other ways. If our understanding and expressions of knowledge are not at least minimally "relational," "perspectival" – "deabsolutized" in that sense – dialogue will proportionally not occur. Only monologue will.

9. Our doctrines and symbols must be constantly reinterpreted to be appropriated – otherwise they become dead museum pieces. Moreover, such reinterpretation will slowly eliminate many apparent contradictions; this of course is an unending task. Still further, the very recognition of this characteristic of doctrines and symbols is in itself very liberating – but also very frightening for some: namely, those who hold power and are reluctant to release it. This constant reinterpretation, and also the recognition of the need of constant reinterpretation, open the door to dialogue. For with the growing awareness of the need for doctrinal and symbolic reinterpretation and appropriation, there burgeons also the awareness of the need for dialogue to fulfill those tasks.

10. We four dialogue partners have different penchants for language that express the need for complete honesty in the dialogue. Starting from a position which assumes that each dialogue partner holds certain of her/his positions with great firmness, some of us have been inclined to use terms like "honesty," "persuade," "confront." The differences among us are partly because we each have a different "feel" for the words involved, but probably even more because we were speaking of different stages in the dialogue and at times had different dialogue participants in mind. We do agree, however, that at the beginning stage of a new dialogue we very much need to stress listening carefully and sympathetically to our partner and the seek our areas of agreement assiduously. At that stage we do not need to "persuade" or "confront," for we had been doing that for decades or even centuries. Our "honesty" at that initial stage must take more the form of listening and stressing commonality so as to work toward balancing out the prior persuading, confronting and stress of differences.

11. And yet, as the dialogue progresses and each side becomes clearer about what the partner really believes and practices, the possibility of arriving at truly contradictory positions has to be reckoned with. At that point we can simply agree to disagree – unless it concerns a threat to human rights. When we are persuaded that that is the case, then we must in conscience confront, oppose in proportional and appropriate ways. Clear examples: the burning of witches by Christians, of widows by Hindus, of Jews by Nazis was to be opposed by all effective means. The decision about what is contradictory and human rights-threatening and who decides to what degree it is, what the most effective response would be, etc. are all related judgments that sometimes are extremely difficult to make, but nevertheless at times cannot be avoided.

12. Because it is rapidly becoming less and less possible to live in isolation – religiously, culturally, economically, politically, physically, etc. – we humans are willy-nilly being forced out of the age of monologue, in which most humans have lived out their lives till now, into the age of dialogue, which is only now dawning. The alternative to dialogue is eventual demise – religious, cultural, economic, political, physical, etc., etc. Since the function of religion/ideology is to provide an explanation of the ultimate meaning of

life, and how to live accordingly, it is incumbent upon all religions/ideologies to lead their constituents into dialogue rather than death.

13. We have learned much in the course of our dialogue here – both because of our commonalities and our differences. We have been forced to think more broadly and deeply and express ourselves more clearly and precisely, and we hope that this will be reflected in our behavior. As a result we are all the more committed to dialogue – and hope that our readers have been helped to move in a similar direction.

The Authors

Leonard Swidler has an STL in Catholic theology, University of Tübingen and a Ph D in history and philosophy, University of Wisconsin. Professor of Catholic Thought and Interreligious Dialogue at Temple University since 1966, he is author or editor of over 40 books and over 130 articles, and Co-founder (1964) and Editor of the *Journal of Ecumenical Studies*. His books include: *Dialogue for Reunion* (1962), *The Ecumenical Vanguard* (1965), *Jewish-Christian Dialogues* (1966), *Buddhism Made Plain* (co-author, 1984), *Toward a Universal Theology of Religion* (1987), *A Jewish-Christian Dialogue on Jesus and Paul* (ed., 1990), *After the Absolute: The Dialogical Future of Religious Reflection* (1990).

John B. Cobb, Jr is Ingraham Professor of Theology at the School of Theology at Claremont and Avery Professor of Religion at the Claremont Graduate School. He is also Director of the Center for Process Studies, which has sponsored a number of East-West dialogues, and the publisher of the journal *Process Studies*. Among his books, *Christ in a Pluralistic Age* and *Beyond Dialogue* are particularly relevant to this discussion. Together with Masao Abe he organized a Buddhist-Christian Encounter group consisting of leading Buddhist thinkers and Christian theologians. He was also the first president of the Society for Buddhist-Christian Studies.

Paul F. Knitter completed his theological studies at the Gregorian University in Rome (1968) and the University of Marburg, Germany (1972). He is working to promote a more effective dialogue between followers of Christianity and of other spiritual paths. He is at present Professor of Theology at Xavier University, Cincinnati. His recent books include: *No Other Name? A Critical Survey of Christian Attitudes toward World Religions* (1985), *The Myth of Christian Uniqueness: Toward a Pluralistic Theology of Religions*, ed. with John Hick (1987) and *Pluralism and Oppression: Theology in World Perspective* (ed., 1990). He also serves as General Editor of Orbis Books' series "Faith Meets Faith" and is active in various Central America peace movements.

Monika K. Hellwig is Professor of Theology at Georgetown University. A longtime participant in Jewish-Christian encounters, and occasional contributor to three-way Jewish-Christian-Muslim conferences, she has been more actively involved in recent years in Christian-Marxist exchanges. She is the author of many articles and contributory chapters as well as more than a dozen books, including *Understanding Catholicism* (Paulist Press, 1981), *Whose Experience Counts in Theological Reflection?* (Marquette University Press, 1982), and *Jesus, the Compassion of God* (Michael Glazier 1983). Her interest in the wider ecumenism has included studies in the Hindu, Buddhist and Islamic traditions of South Asia.